THE LAZY
FUNDAMENTAL
ANALYST

THE LAZY FUNDAMENTAL ANALYST

APPLYING QUANTITATIVE TECHNIQUES TO FUNDAMENTAL STOCK ANALYSIS

FRED PIARD

Hh

HARRIMAN HOUSE LTD

18 College Street
Petersfield
Hampshire
GU31 4AD
GREAT BRITAIN

Tel: +44 (0)1730 233870
Email: enquiries@harriman-house.com
Website: www.harriman-house.com

First published in Great Britain in 2014

ISBN: 9780857193964

British Library Cataloguing in Publication Data
A CIP catalogue record for this book can be obtained from the British Library.

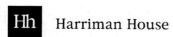 Harriman House

CONTENTS

DISCLAIMER

The information provided in this book is for educational purposes only. It is not investment advice. Before deciding to invest in financial markets you should carefully consider your investment objectives, level of experience and risk appetite. The possibility exists that you could sustain a loss of some or all of your initial investment. You should seek advice from an independent financial advisor if you have any doubts.

All products, ETPs, indexes, tools and websites quoted in this book are the property and trademarks of their respective issuers. This work provides information about various investment methods. It does not constitute an offer, a financial promotion or a solicitation to purchase or sell any financial instruments.

No representation is being made that any investor will achieve results similar to those discussed here. The past performance of a system or methodology is not necessarily indicative for the future. The results presented in this book are mostly based on simulations. They have been made as realistic as possible. However there is a risk of errors from the data, software and the human operator.

CFTC rule 4.41 – hypothetical or simulated performance results have certain limitations. Unlike an actual performance record, simulated results do not represent actual trading. Also, since the trades have not been executed, the results may have under- or overcompensated for the impact, if any, of certain market factors, such as lack of liquidity. Simulated trading programs in general are also subject to the fact that they are designed with the benefit of hindsight. No representation is being made that any account will or is likely to achieve profit or losses similar to those shown.

THE AUTHOR

Fred Piard gained extensive experience in the software industry, information systems consulting and marketing before discovering an interest in the financial markets. Self-taught in this field, he puts into practice what he learnt from his previous activities to build his own methodology. From his years in research he has the ability to combine a systemic point of view and an analytic approach. As a software architect he knows that the things that work the best in the long term are the simplest. As a consultant he has experienced the real economy through various sectors: energy, banking, health care, manufacturing and public administration. And he has learned from marketing that human group behaviour can sometimes be modelled, but never predicted. Fred provides systematic portfolio strategies for investors and professionals. His proprietary library of models on themes and sectors can be personalised for specific requirements. He has a PhD in computer science, an MSc in software engineering and an MSc in civil engineering.

LIKE US, ADD US, FOLLOW US

www.facebook.com/harrimanhouse

@harrimanhouse

www.linkedin.com/company/harriman-house

www.harriman-house.com

FREE EBOOK EDITION

As a buyer of the print edition of *The Lazy Fundamental Analyst* you can now download the eBook edition free of charge to read on an eBook reader, smartphone or computer. Simply go to:

http://ebooks.harriman-house.com/lazyfundamentalanalyst

or point your smartphone at the QRC below.

You can then register and download your free eBook.

PREFACE

WHAT THE BOOK COVERS

This book contains a collection of investing strategies based on the application of quantitative analysis to fundamental factors. The strategies are classified by sector and market capitalisation (for the latter, the indexes used are: S&P 500, Russell 2000 and DJ 30).

All the strategies share some common characteristics:

- They are the result of an **extensive statistical study** on 15 years of historical data, and are also validated by **common sense.**

- They are **100% fundamental:** no use is made of chart analysis or technical indicators.

- They use **only US stocks and ETFs.** The concepts may well work in other markets but no representation is made about the expected results.

WHO THIS BOOK IS FOR

This book was written for anyone looking for simple, effective and low-risk investing strategies. The strategies described in the following pages can be managed in just a few minutes per month, making them suitable, for example, for investors with a full-time job.

The book is designed to be short, simple and actionable. No specific background in finance or statistics is needed. However, the understanding and implementation of the strategies needs a logical mind and the ability to feel comfortable with browsing online financial data sources.

STRUCTURE OF THE BOOK

The book consists of three parts.

The first part gives the information that readers need to understand how strategies have been designed and evaluated. It also details a portfolio protection method that may be added to any stock strategy to minimise the impact of market downturns.

The second part of the book, and the most important, is organised by 10 sectors. For each sector a strategy is proposed for large capitalisations (companies in the S&P 500 Index) and another one for small capitalisations (companies in the Russell 2000 Index). Mega caps (DJ 30 companies) are treated independently in a separate chapter. Each strategy is then compared to specialised sector indexes.

The final part shows some applications of the strategies introduced in the second part, in particular mixing strategies and top-down analysis.

INTRODUCTION

My first active experience in the financial market was to buy shares in a company and a tracker. Then I forgot them for three years. I was lucky enough that my profit on the company just about offset my loss on the tracker – but I was aware that it was just luck. So I decided to follow the People Who Know. I tried half a dozen paid services. The result of my follow-the-gurus period was no better than when I started.

The next stage was to study some technical indicators and patterns, buy software with configurable trading signals, and have a go at day trading. It involved a lot of time and stress. It also conflicted with my lifestyle – I like the idea of putting money to work for one's life, not the opposite.

I found a better way when I began to scan with screeners and use simulation tools on the history of fundamental and technical data for thousands of stocks and ETFs. I discovered that it was possible to find good strategies that involved trading just once a month; these strategies ignored charts and the news, and removed much of the doubt and emotion.

This book is a result of those early studies which are, in effect, a simplified approach to fundamental analysis.

It may be useful to take a quick look at what we mean by fundamental analysis. A common definition of fundamental analysis is as follows:

> Fundamental analysis of a business involves analysing its financial statements and health, its management and competitive advantages, and its competitors and markets.

Professional analysts undertake comprehensive due diligence before buying or recommending a stock. Their study includes financial statements, products and services, market trend, executives' track records, legal environment, competition, partners, possible mergers and acquisitions, foreseeable events, etc. Some elements are quantitative, others are qualitative, and sometimes subjective. Such comprehensive due diligence needs a lot of work.

1

Most investors have neither the skills, nor the time, to perform this work. Moreover, even extensive due diligence is not a guarantee of investing success. Some erroneous data, misinterpretation, undisclosed information or unpredictable event can transform the perfect stock pick into an investor's nightmare. This is what is called *idiosyncratic risk* in portfolio management: the risk linked to a special situation in a specific company.

My aim in this book is to offer a "lazy" approach to fundamental analysis, based on two principles: quantitative selection and diversification. I will show you how to choose stocks blindly, taking into account only a couple of financial ratios. Each analysis will not result in one stock pick, but at least ten. This is a minimum portfolio size to absorb most of the idiosyncratic risk and also the additional risk carried by the "laziness" of this methodology.

The strategies presented in this book are simplified versions inspired from my library of adaptable investing models. They are so simple that they may be managed in a couple of minutes every month using an appropriate stock screener. Each one is simulated on 15 years of historical data. Past performances are not a guarantee for the future, but their consistency will show you that this approach is not only lazy and simple, but I hope also smart.

My previous book, *Quantitative Investing* (Harriman House, 2013), was focused on ETF strategies using tactical allocation and seasonal patterns. This one is exclusively about stocks and fundamental analysis. Together, they constitute a comprehensive reference to build and manage robust portfolios.

PART I

METHODOLOGY

CHAPTER 1

QUANTITATIVE FUNDAMENTAL ANALYSIS

This chapter is a quick introduction to quantitative fundamental analysis. The focus is on keeping things simple and practical.

OBJECTIVES

If fundamental analysis needs a lot of time and specific skills, is it completely out of reach for most investors?

Short answer: no. There is another way to use the fundamental data on companies: quantitative investing. This is a scientific approach based on hypotheses and empirical testing that has been developed by sophisticated funds, but some techniques are also perfectly feasible for individual investors.

Here is my definition of quantitative investing:

> Identifying reasonable and measurable hypotheses about behaviours of the financial market so as to make investment decisions with an acceptable confidence in expected returns and risks.

Taking into account only numerical information and processing it in a systematic way makes the investment process independent of opinions and emotions. It also makes it reproducible by anyone at any time.

My first book, *Quantitative Investing*, showed that a quantitative approach doesn't need to be complicated to offer investors an edge in the market. This book extends the possibilities in another direction – it provides 20 simple strategies that have been profitable for 15 years. They are based on ranking and filtering stocks using fundamental factors such as valuation and growth ratios. Each strategy can be managed in just a few minutes per month without being a financial or mathematical expert. A summary of the performance of the 20 strategies is given in Appendix 2.

Readers may find different applications for the information included in this book, for example:

- Picking strategies according to a personal interest in specific sectors.

- Combining the strategies (described in Part III).

- Using lists of factors (later defined "individually relevant factors") as a starting point to design your own strategies, or simply to understand what works in each sector.

- Understanding better the relationships between return and risk across all sectors.

THE ART OF BACKTESTING

For an investor, it is not so important to know if some fundamental factors, such as the price-earnings ratio, the sales growth rate, or others, can help in telling what a company is worth. What is important is if they are accurate in anticipating flows of institutional money that may move the share price in the near future.

Designing a quantitative fundamental model involves identifying states of fundamental factors that may predict an increase in share price with a high probability. The best way we have to do this is to look for patterns in the past. This process requires model simulations on historical data, also called backtesting. However, the process of simulating an investing strategy in the past has some risks.

First, a simulation must only use data that would have been available at the time of the decision process. In particular:

1. It must include no longer existing and merged companies.
2. Index-based universes of stocks must be timestamped. For example, the list of S&P 500 companies is not the same today as it was a year ago.

3. The fundamental data must be correctly timestamped and available at the specified date.

The database I use in this study complies with these conditions.

LIQUIDITY

Another danger is that simulations often give unrealistic results for low-liquidity stocks, because the volume of transactions may be insufficient to build a sizeable position. Even if that is not the case, the bid/ask spread and the order book structure sometimes give a real price which varies by 5%, 10%, or more, from the theoretical simulated price.

Funds are often forced by their own rules to trade in index-based universes so that a minimum liquidity is guaranteed. The strategies presented in this book are limited to stocks belonging to major indexes, so liquidity, in general, should not be a problem. However, using limit orders is always recommended, especially for small capitalisation stocks.

TRADING COSTS

Simulation sometimes underestimates trading costs. Realistic costs are taken into account here. You will see only strategies rebalanced every four weeks, which minimises the impact of trading costs. Nevertheless, the commission on the same order may vary widely depending on the broker – needless to say this can affect performance! I have no interest in advertising for any broker – compare what is on offer and feel free to change brokers or to open a second account.

SHORT-SELLING

Simulation of short-selling strategies are also very tricky. The only market where buying and selling are symmetric actions is forex. Buying a currency is selling another one. But short selling a stock is not a similar operation to buying it. You have to borrow the stock; the cost of doing so depends on your broker and can vary over time. The continued availability of the borrowed stock is not guaranteed for the retail investor. Your broker has the right to ask you – at any time – to buy them back. If you cannot do it yourself, the order is automatically forced.

Short-selling strategies cannot be simulated in a reliable way, simply because the required data don't exist. To my knowledge there is no database available to retail investors that can tell you that a stock S was shortable by a broker B from a date D1 to a date D2, with an average borrowing rate R. This is one of the reasons why there is no short selling of individual stocks in this book.

OVERFITTING AND DATA MINING

In statistics and machine learning, overfitting occurs when a model interprets randomness as a relationship between data. According to Wikipedia:

> Overfitting generally occurs when a model is excessively complex, such as having too many parameters relative to the number of observations.

The consequence of overfitting is to believe that a model is better than it is in reality. The rules, parameter values, simulation interval, start date and number of positions may be unwittingly optimised for a particular market situation. It is easy to optimise simulations by complicating the model. But the more complicated the model, the less likely the results may be replicated.

There is no absolute guarantee against overfitting. However, good practice can reduce the risk. The best guards are simplicity and common sense. Warren Buffett has written that we should invest only in what we can understand. That is true for individual stocks and it is also true for strategies.

All strategies in this book are very simple. Each of them is defined by only two variable parameters, which are two fundamental factors. The other parameters are constants: sectors, stock indexes, number of holdings, position sizes, transaction costs. This addresses the two first points in the definition above: complexity and parameters. The third point is the number of observations. Here, most strategies are rebalanced every four weeks over 15 years. Simulations have 13 x 15 = 195 rebalancing dates. As there are at least 10 holdings in each portfolio, it means at least 1950 elementary observations by model.

In addition, I consider that a reasonable simulation should contain at least a bull period, a bear period and a sideways period in the study interval. Here, simulations run through two stock market cycles since 1999. Returns are calculated on three, five-year periods to evaluate their consistency. Getting positive returns on all periods is not a guarantee against overfitting, but it is a clue that, even if there is overfitting, it doesn't have disastrous effects in certain market conditions.

Eventually, the best protection against overfitting is to bet on various models based on different logic. My recommendation for building an all-weather portfolio is to blend models based on various rationales like tactical allocation, seasonal patterns and fundamental factors.

THE LUCK FACTOR

A simulation makes sense if the data are sufficient in quantity and quality to make a good mathematical model. But even with a perfect mathematical model, the precise sequence of losses and gains can lead to very different results. Scientists call that non-ergodicity, gamblers just call it luck.

To give an example, imagine a game where your odds to win are 57% and if you win, you gain $1, if you lose, you lose $1. Mathematically it is a profitable game, but the trajectory of an individual gambler can take quite different paths. Fig 1.1 gives an idea of possible paths depending on the sequence of gains and losses:

Fig 1.1: Possible paths for the same probabilistic game

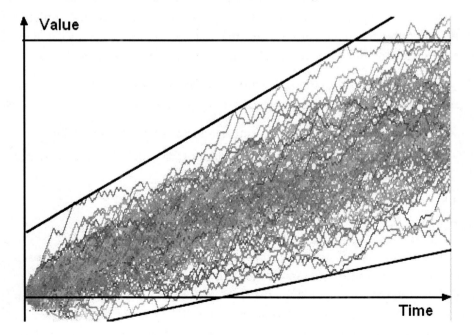

If you consider an investing strategy as a game, the probability of winning and the win-loss ratio may be overrated because of a methodological mistake or a too small data sample. In this case, the beam representing possible futures for the portfolio value may be wider than you think. The wider the beam, the less certain the profitability.

Using reasonably good models and testing them on a period of 15 years gives us an edge, not a guarantee.

A SECTOR-ORIENTED ANALYSIS

Most investing books treat fundamental factors the same way for all sectors and industries. In reality, professional analysts know that fundamental factors don't have the same significance for all industries and all business models.

To take an example: the case of debt ratios in real estate investment trusts (REIT). For most industries, debt is a negative element; for REITs debt is at the core of the business model. They make profits by leveraging capital, investing in real estate and playing with rates. Other categories of financial companies like BDC (Business Development Companies) may also make a profit by leveraging capital. For such companies, debt ratios are much higher than in other companies and it is normal. Of course, any company can have too much debt and an extreme debt ratio is always a warning signal.

More generally, using the same fundamental factors for all companies, regardless of their business, may have two consequences:

1.   Systematically eliminating entire industries from the portfolio.
2.   From time to time selecting companies for which the factors are not relevant.

So, this book is sector-oriented.

But which sectors?

Investors can refer to various stock market taxonomies. The two most used are the Global Industry Classification Standard (GICS®) by Morgan Stanley Capital International and Standard & Poor's, and the Industry Classification Benchmark (ICB) by FTSE International. The GICS is structured in 10 sectors, 24 industry groups, 68 industries and 154 sub-industries. The ICB is partitioned into 10 industries, 19 supersectors, 41 sectors and 114 subsectors. The top levels of both classifications have 10 categories and similarities, but are not equivalent.

I made the choice to differentiate companies using the GICS sectors: Consumer Discretionary, Consumer Staples, Energy, Financials, Health Care, Industrials, Information Technology, Materials, Telecommunication Services and Utilities. Each of these will be defined later.

CHAPTER 2

STRATEGY DESIGN AND EVALUATION

This chapter first defines the fundamental factors that will be used in this book's strategies and then the criteria to evaluate them. It also lists the tools and requirements to execute the strategies. Finally, it ends with a brief overview of the hypotheses, vocabulary and formalisms used in the book.

FUNDAMENTAL FACTORS

WORKING LIST

I have looked for relationships between sectors and quantitative fundamental factors, focusing my study on two indexes corresponding to market capitalisation segments: the S&P 500 Index for large capitalisations and the Russell 2000 Index for small caps.

Famous investors like Graham, Buffett, Zweig, Greenblatt, Piotroski, O'Neil and others have extensively covered the topic of stock valuation using fundamental factors. I suggest you refer to these sources if you want to learn more about quantitative fundamental analysis.

I have limited my work to fundamental factors available in various free or low-cost screeners. The reason is that I don't want my investing strategies to depend on a specific screener or software. In my opinion, being an independent investor means, first, being independent of tools.

Experts may be annoyed by missing a few of their favourite ratios, but this limitation also has positive side-effects. It forced me to keep things simple and to use factors that are recognised as the most important by consensus.

Table 2.1 lists the factors with their explicit full names, the symbol I will use later, and their names in Finviz and Portfolio123 (explained later). You can probably also find them in other tools.

Table 2.1: Working list of fundamental factors (TTM = trailing 12 months)

Full name	Symbol	FINVIZ	P123
Price To Earnings Ratio Including Extraordinary Items, TTM	PE	P/E	PEInclXorTTM
Next Year Projected PE Ratio	FPE	Forward P/E	ProjPENextFY
Price/Earnings to Next Year Growth Rate	PEG	PEG	PEG
Price to Sales Ratio, TTM	PS	P/S	Pr2SalesTTM
Price to Book Ratio, Last Quarter	PB	P/B	Pr2BookQ
Price To Free Cash Flow Per Share Ratio, TTM	PFCF	Price/Free Cash Flow	Pr2FrCashFlTTM
EPS Growth Rate, TTM over prior TTM (%)	EPSG1Y	EPS growth this year	EPS%ChgTTM
Sales Growth Rate, 5 Year (%)	SG5Y	Sales growth past 5 years	Sales5YCGr%
Sales Growth Rate, Last Quarter vs. Prior Quarter (%)	SG1Q	Sales growth qtr over qtr	Sales%ChgPQ
Return on Assets, TTM (%)	ROA	Return on Assets TTM	ROA%TTM
Return on Average Common Equity, TTM (%)	ROE	Return on Equity	ROE%TTM
Current Ratio, Last Quarter	CR	Current Ratio	CurRatioQ
Gross Margin, TTM (%)	GM	Gross Margin	GMgn%TTM
Net Profit Margin, TTM (%)	NPM	Net Profit Margin	NPMgn%TTM
Payout Ratio, TTM (%)	POR	Payout Ratio	PayRatioTTM
Institutional Percent Owned (%)	INST	Institutional Ownership	Inst%Own

These indicators can be grouped into five categories:

1. *Valuation*: PE, FPE, PEG, PS, PB, PFCF
2. *Growth*: EPSG1, SG5Y, SG1Q

3. *Profitability*: ROE, ROA, GM, NPM

4. *Financial strength*: CR, POR

5. *Ownership*: INST

Depending on the factor, the best values may be the highest or the lowest numbers.

- **valuation** factors: lower is usually better

- **growth and profitability** factors: higher is better

- **current ratio** (CR): higher is better

- **payout ratio** (POR): the better may be the higher or the lower depending on the reference set. In some categories of stocks, the market favours companies using their profit to pay shareholders, in other categories those reinvesting in their business are preferred.

For institutional ownership (INST), when it has an influence, lower is better. We can interpret it as a sign of companies that are less invested by institutions, and whose share price may appreciate by attracting institutional capital in the future.

I won't go into further detail on any of the above ratios – it is not necessary for the purposes of understanding and executing the strategies described later.

INDIVIDUALLY RELEVANT FACTORS FOR A REFERENCE SET OF STOCKS

I define each sector in each index as a reference set of stocks. To illustrate this idea, the health care sector in the S&P 500 is a reference set, financials in the Russell 2000 is another one.

For each reference set, I have looked for the fundamental factors within the working list that are relevant when used alone. I will shortly describe the methodology defining what I mean by "relevant when used alone", or "individually relevant".

For each reference set and each factor in the working list, I have created two portfolios:

1. a monthly rebalanced portfolio holding the 10 stocks with the **highest** values of the factor, and

2. a monthly rebalanced portfolio holding the 10 stocks with the **lowest** values.

Then I have compared the 15-year returns of both portfolios and the reference set (for example the return of the whole health care sector in the S&P 500). The portfolio and the reference set are equal-weight for this calculation.

I consider the factor as individually relevant if:

1. The difference in annualised returns between both portfolios is 5% or more, and

2. The best of both portfolios has a better annualised return than the reference set.

When a factor is not listed as individually relevant, it doesn't mean that it is not relevant at all: it is only a claim that it doesn't make a significant statistical difference when used alone. Nevertheless, it may make a difference in combination with other factors.

In the second part of the book, individually relevant factors are listed for each reference set, then a strategy is proposed. Strategies are designed to be implemented as they are described. Knowing individually relevant factors is not necessary to implement them. I give the individually relevant factors because I think it may help advanced readers wanting to design and backtest their own strategies, with Portfolio123 or another tool. It may also be of interest if you just want to know some of the factors that work best in each sector.

The strategy for each reference set is based on an individually relevant factor and often a second factor, which is not necessarily individually relevant. The choice of factors is the result of testing. The whole process of factor testing and selection is not described here.

TOOLS

To execute any of the strategies described in the second part requires:

1. getting a list of all the stocks in a sector and a given index (the S&P 500 or the Russell 2000), and

2. sorting them regarding given fundamental factors from the working list.

All the required information is available for free on the internet. However doing the job manually might require a few hours, whereas with the appropriate tools it is just a matter of minutes, if not seconds.

Some advanced tools provided by brokers may fulfil the requirements. If you have access to software or an online platform from your broker, this is the first place to look at.

If you don't have access to such a tool, do an online search for "stock screener". As the list and functions of available screeners change over time, making a survey yourself may be useful. Some screeners don't allow you to sort a list on all factors, but do allow the list to be exported in a spreadsheet format and to select the factors to put in the file. Then it is easy to sort the records on any column. Among the free online screeners, **Finviz.com** can do this. The process to use Finviz this way has six steps:

1. Create a "custom view".
2. Select the data to export in the "settings".
3. Create a screen corresponding to the strategy using the "filters".
4. Export and download the table in a csv file.
5. Import the file to a spreadsheet.
6. Rank and select the stocks using the right factors.

Fig. 2.1: Personalising a Finviz screen for a strategy (the "export" link is below the table)

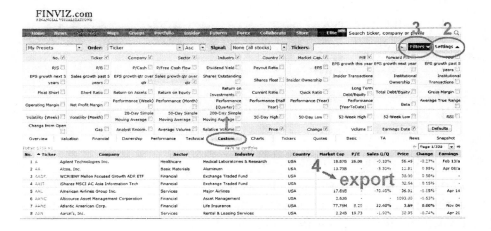

This is straightforward for large cap strategies and for some sectors; unfortunately there is no Russell 2000 filter and Finviz sector classification doesn't match exactly the GICS standard.

Finviz is a great tool, but I prefer using Portfolio123 for this purpose: once the right parameters are entered, the stock selection is much faster. It contains a sophisticated screener that can obtain the current holdings of any of my strategies in just a click. An extended free trial and the code of strategies is available following instructions here: **stratecode.com**

EVALUATING STRATEGIES

In the second part of this book, each strategy is presented with a 15-year simulation report including a table of statistical analysis and a chart. Simulations longer than 15 years would not be very useful. Indeed, what interests us is the ratios that have worked in recent times, not 50 years ago. 15 years including two bear markets is a long enough period to give an idea of what can happen in all market conditions.

It is helpful to understand the criteria used to evaluate and compare strategies in terms of profitability and risk, but it is not necessary to understand everything to implement them. In case you find this section too complicated, just skip it and try to read it again after finishing the rest of the book.

The eight evaluation tools we'll be looking at are:

1. Total return
2. Annualised return
3. Max drawdown
4. Standard deviation
5. Benchmark
6. Sharpe ratio
7. Sortino ratio
8. Correlation with benchmark

I briefly explain these statistical measures below in the context of the book's analysis; but for more detailed explanations please refer to statistics textbooks (Wikipedia also has good articles on these).

1. TOTAL RETURN

The total return is the actual rate of return of an investment over a given period. In the case of a stock portfolio, it includes capital gains and dividends. For dynamic portfolios like those in the book, dividends are reinvested in shares. The hypothesis is made that shares are fractionable.

For example, if $100 invested in a strategy becomes $249 after a few years (including dividends reinvested), the total return is the final value minus the initial value, divided by the initial value: (249 − 100) / 100 = 1.49 or 149%.

2. ANNUALISED RETURN

Annualised return in this book means the Compound Annual Growth Rate (CAGR).

If the total return of a period of Q years is T%, the CAGR is:

$$CAGR = (1+(T/100))^{1/Q} - 1$$

In other words, it is the hypothetical constant annual return that would have given the total return. The purpose of annualised returns is to standardise return measurement to enable comparison of various investments over different time periods.

For example, let's suppose that a strategy has a 50% total return over two years. It's CAGR is 0.225 (22.5%).

To see how this works, let's assume the strategy starts with $100:

1. In the first year this increases to $122.5 ($100 + ($100 x 22.5%))
2. In the second year this increases to $150 ($122.5 + ($122.5 x 22.5%))

If a strategy multiplied capital by 10 in 10 years (+900%), the CAGR is 25.9%.

The number of years does not need to be whole number; the CAGR may be calculated on only six months if you wish. Of course, a CAGR calculated for a short period has little significance regarding a strategy's performance.

An annualised return on a long period is an imprecise indicator. When evaluating a strategy, I take the time to calculate it for several sub-periods.

The variations help to understand the behaviour in different market conditions.

3. MAX DRAWDOWN

The drawdown is sometimes defined as "the decline in value from a peak to a bottom". However things are not so simple: *which peak* and *which bottom*?

First I will define the drawdown at the present time, then in the past, then define the *maximum drawdown*, which is really the concept of interest.

The current value of drawdown is usually defined as the loss in percentage terms between the highest portfolio value and the current portfolio value. For example, if the highest value of a strategy portfolio was 500,000 and the current value is 450,000, the drawdown is:

$$(50-45)/50 = 0.1 = 10\%$$

By definition, if the current value is at its highest point, the drawdown is zero.

The drawdown at a date in the past is the loss in percentage between the highest value before or at this date, and the value at this date.

The *max drawdown* for a period of time is the maximum of the drawdowns for all dates in the period.

If we define the drawdown at a time t as a mathematical function DD(t) and the max drawdown as another function MDD(t), then:

$$MDD(t) = max (MDD(t-1), DD(t))$$

The max drawdown at time t is the maximum of its own value at time t-1, and of the drawdown at time t. In finance, time is discrete: the variable t is an integer. It may measure any time unit in your charting tool, from minute to year.

In this book max drawdowns are calculated using the daily low. Be careful when reading books and articles, sometimes max drawdowns are calculated using weekly or monthly close prices, which may be quite inaccurate for representing what really happens to a portfolio.

An important detail about a drawdown is the gain necessary to recover it.

If the drawdown is x, it is:

$x/(1-x)$

For example: when a portfolio has a 30% drawdown, it needs a 43% gain to recover:

$0.30/(1-0.30) = 0.428$

When it has a 50% drawdown, it needs a 100% gain:

$0.5/(1-0.5) = 1$

The max drawdown is an important concept. Some strategies are profitable in theory, but not feasible because the possible max drawdown may go beyond the available capital. For example, the Martingale system of doubling up after every loss. It works in theory with an infinite capital, in practice the gambler (or trader) will eventually be bankrupted. The same may happen when leveraging a profitable strategy.

4. STANDARD DEVIATION

The standard deviation (Std) measures the dispersion of a data set. In finance, it is usually calculated for a time series of returns as a measure of historic volatility. In effect, it is used to quantify the *risk* of an investment.

If R1...Rn is the series of returns and A is average return, then:

$Std = \sqrt{(((R1-A)^2+(R2-A)^2+...+(Rn-A)^2)/n)}$

The closer the period returns stay to the average, the lower the standard deviation and the safer the strategy (if the return is positive).

The standard deviation is used in the calculation of the Sharpe and Sortino ratios, defined hereafter.

5. BENCHMARK

A *benchmark* is an index for comparative reference. In Part II, unless otherwise specified, the benchmark for all strategies, whatever the sector and market cap segment, will be the SPDR S&P 500 ETF Trust (ticker: SPY). It tracks the

S&P 500 Index, with dividends. Some readers might prefer the Russell 2000 Index as a benchmark for small caps, but I want to keep things as simple and pragmatic as possible.

6. SHARPE RATIO

The Sharpe ratio is a risk-adjusted performance indicator: the higher, the better.

The idea of the Sharpe ratio is to evaluate the expected return by unit of risk. The expected return is measured by the annualised return on an arbitrary period, the risk by the historic volatility on the same period. The return used by Sharpe was first defined as absolute, then later as relative to a benchmark.

The most common formula takes the annualised return of an investment (<R>) minus the benchmark annualised return (Ro), then divides it by the standard deviation of the excess return (Std):

(<R>-Ro)/Std

When it is used for stock strategies, the benchmark is often a major stock index like the S&P 500.

For a given average return, the lower the standard deviation, the higher the Sharpe ratio. It is interpreted as a better chance to obtain the expected return in the future. The Sharpe ratio promotes strategies that have good *and* steady returns.

As an example, let's take two investments X1 and X2 for a given period.

- X1 has a 20% annualised return and an Std of 30%.
- X2 has a 10% annualised return and an Std of 10%.
- For the same period, the benchmark has returned 0%.

In this case, Sharpe's formula considers X2 as better than X1. It tells us that the higher return of X1 is not worth the additional risk. It is also a clue that we can find leveraging factors for X2 so as to obtain either a better expected return than X1 for the same risk, or a lower risk for the same expected return.

7. SORTINO RATIO

The drawback of the Sharpe ratio is that it penalises strategies that sometimes have exceptionally good periods. Exceptional periods, good or bad, increase the standard deviation. The Sortino ratio corrects that, taking into account only the negative volatility. Periods with a return above the benchmark are excluded from the calculation, so they don't penalise the Sortino ratio.

8. CORRELATION WITH BENCHMARK

Correlation is a statistical measure of the closeness of returns of two data series. It usually varies between -1 and +1: the closer to 1, the higher the correlation, while the closer to -1, the greater the inverse correlation. The correlation with a benchmark points out how a strategy is influenced by broad market moves. This information may be used in advanced portfolio management.

LIMITS ON EVALUATION

Strategies can be evaluated and compared if they can be simulated on a long enough period, and with a set of sufficient decision points (trades), covering various market conditions. The longer the period, the better the evaluation. However, even with statistics over 15 years figures should always be treated with caution. A difference of 1% in annualised return between two strategies may be random.

These criteria give an edge, not a guarantee. Past performance, simulated *or real*, is never a guarantee of the future.

ASSUMPTIONS, VOCABULARY AND PRESENTATION

Unless otherwise stated, all the strategies and simulations in this book share the following characteristics:

- Orders are simulated on open price.
- The data used for calculations and trade decisions are the data available after the market close the day before.
- Gains and dividends are reinvested.

I call *rebalancing* the double action of making a decision to change (or not) holdings in a portfolio, and changing the position sizes in a portfolio (generally to keep an equal weight).

For all simulations in Part II, all positions are reset in equal weight on every rebalancing date. In real portfolio management, my advice is to buy in equal weight the new positions, and to adjust other position sizes when the difference between the largest and the smallest positions value goes beyond 15%. Doing so, the impact of trading costs can be reduced.

I will mainly describe strategies where portfolios are rebalanced every four weeks.

All dates use the US format (i.e. mm/dd/yyyy).

STRATEGY DEFINITION

Strategies are described with the table format shown in Table 2.2.

Table 2.2: Generic strategy description

Name	Strategy name used in the book
Index	The set of companies from which the stocks are selected
Sector	Sector of activity from which the stocks are selected
Rebalanced	Rebalancing period (usually four weeks)
Positions	Number of positions (it will usually be 10 for large caps, 20 for small caps)
Maximum size	Maximum part of the portfolio invested in a single position (usually 10% for large caps, 5% for small caps)
Rules	List of selection rules
Transaction costs	Percentage of invested capital used in simulation to model commission and bid-ask spread. 0.2% for large companies, 0.5% for small caps. Limit orders are recommended.

The results of simulations are summarised by statistical data and a chart representing the portfolio total return (%) in time. In simulation reports, all numerical data have two decimals. In the text and tables, returns, drawdowns and standard deviations are given without decimals; Sharpe and Sortino ratios are given with a decimal. A higher precision is not necessary for evaluating an expected performance.

The "Turnover" data represents the percentage of stocks changing on each rebalancing date.

There is no survivor bias and no look-ahead bias in simulations. This means that at each point in time:

- Subsequently extinct and merged companies can be selected and be part of the simulations.
- The changes in index composition are taken into account.
- The fundamental factors were available in real time.

CHAPTER 3

PORTFOLIO PROTECTION

How to protect a stock portfolio from market downturns is not the core of this book. However, I think it would not be complete without addressing the subject. This chapter proposes a protection tactic. In Part II, every strategy will be simulated first unprotected, then adding this tactic.

MARKET TIMING

Market timing involves anticipating trends. It is a science and an art in which many indicators may be used: price moving averages, put/call ratios of options, sentiment surveys, etc.

Indicators are used to determine if the market is likely to go up (bullish signal), or down (bearish signal). Some methods are better than others, but there is no perfect one, they all give erroneous signals from time to time. They are supposed to work statistically over the long term. I propose to combine two indicators.

1. EPS ESTIMATE MOMENTUM

My first indicator "EPS Estimate Momentum" is an aggregate fundamental ratio over the S&P 500 Index. It gives a bearish signal when the S&P 500 current year EPS estimate is below its own value three months previously, and a bullish signal when it is above this value. This data is provided in various data feeds and tools, among them Portfolio123. It is generally updated once a week. It is an indicator of what is anticipated for the real economy until the end of the current year.

2. UNEMPLOYMENT MOMENTUM

The second indicator "Unemployment Momentum" is macroeconomic. It gives a bearish signal when the US unemployment rate is above its own value three months ago, and a bullish signal when it is below this value. The US unemployment rate is published once a month, usually in the first half of the month for the previous month. It is widely broadcasted on financial and news websites. Unemployment is a powerful indicator because it is at the same time a barometer of activity in the real economy and an anticipation of overall sentiment.

COMBINING THE TWO INDICATORS

Table 3.1 compares the performance of a portfolio that is long the S&P 500 Index:

1. 100% of the time
2. when Unemployment Momentum is bullish
3. when EPS Estimate Momentum is bullish
4. when at least one indicator is bullish
5. when both indicators are bullish simultaneously

The rest of the time, it is in cash. Timing indicators are checked every four weeks and the period studied is Feb 1999 to Jan 2014. Dividends are included.

Table 3.1: Market timing performances

Timing	Annualised return	Drawdown	Volatility
Buy and hold	5%	-55%	20%
Unemployment bullish	11%	-24%	13%
EPS estimate bullish	9%	-20%	12%
One is bullish	12%	-29%	15%
Two are bullish	8%	-11%	10%

The best return is obtained with the "optimistic" combination (one indicator bullish at least). The lowest risk in terms of volatility and drawdown is the "pessimistic" combination (both indicators bullish). Starting from here, I will always apply the optimistic combination.

FROM MARKET TIMING TO HEDGING

The best known use of market timing is to sell a portfolio and go to cash every time a bearish signal occurs, and buy again on the next bullish signal. It has four main drawbacks:

1. Cutting the income stream for dividend-oriented investors.

2. Transaction costs: the more holdings there are, the more expensive it is.

3. Tax implications of capital gains that we may not want to make at the moment.

4. A psychological bias being out of the market: buying back in is a difficult decision.

Hedging can be a better alternative. The proposition is to take a short position in the S&P 500 when my two indicators are bearish. This is supposed to offset part, or all, of the loss on the equity portfolio in a market downturn. But there is an inconvenience: buying a hedge needs either to reduce the stock holdings, or to use margin. The first case implies a potential loss in performance, the second one an additional borrowing cost.

Sophisticated investors usually hedge with futures contracts and options. Hedging with futures is not possible for any portfolio size, and managing options needs time and skill. For individual investors, ETFs are the simplest solution. All hedged simulations hereafter use a short position in SPY sized at 100% of the stock holdings value, and a 2% annual carry cost.

You can also consider buying an inverse ETF like SH (ProShares Short S&P 500 ETF). And you may prefer hedging small cap strategies with the Russell 2000. I make the choice of the S&P 500 for all strategies to keep things simple. It also works better over the period of study.

In Appendix 1 you can find additional information on hedging with leveraged ETFs.

PART I SUMMARY

- This book explains investment strategies on stocks based on fundamental factors.

- They are simple enough to be executed in a few minutes per month by an individual investor.

- The criteria to evaluate strategies are defined.

- The fundamental factors to be used are listed.

- The tools, vocabulary, assumptions and generic presentation of a strategy are described.

- The concepts of market timing and hedging are introduced to present portfolio protection tactics.

The second part will explore the US stock market sector by sector, list for each sector the most relevant fundamental factors, describe strategies and show their simulated performance on 15 years of historical data.

PART II

SECTOR ANALYSIS

INTRODUCTION

This second part has one chapter for each GICS sector. The format of each chapter is the same and is as follows:

- Each chapter begins with the sector's definition and gives as examples its largest companies.

- Then two following sections correspond to companies in the S&P 500 and the Russell 2000.

- For each reference set, the individually relevant factors are listed and a strategy is proposed. Each strategy is simulated on 15 years without, then with, hedging. The hedging tactics have been previously discussed.

- The performance consistency is evaluated through three, five-year periods, and is followed by a short comment.

There are 10 sectors, therefore 10 chapters, and an eleventh chapter about the Dow Jones Industrial Average. The last chapter of this part compares the strategies with two series of sector ETFs.

CHAPTER 4

CONSUMER DISCRETIONARY

SECTOR OVERVIEW

DEFINITION

The definition given by Morgan Stanley Capital International (MSCI) and Standard & Poor's in their Global Industry Classification Standard (GICS®) is:

> The Consumer Discretionary Sector encompasses those businesses that tend to be the most sensitive to economic cycles. Its manufacturing segment includes automotive, household durable goods, leisure equipment, and textiles & apparel. The services segment includes hotels, restaurants and other leisure facilities, media production and services, and consumer retailing and services.

COMPANIES

This sector contains 84 companies in the S&P 500 and 259 in the Russell 2000, making it the largest for large caps. Table 4.1 gives the 10 largest companies in the sector by market capitalisation at the time of writing. Depending on share price relative moves, the list may have changed when you read this.

Table 4.1: 10 largest companies in the S&P 500 Consumer Discretionary sector

Ticker	Name	Industry
AMZN	Amazon.com Inc	Internet & Catalog Retail
CMCSA	Comcast Corp	Media
DIS	Walt Disney Co (The)	Media
F	Ford Motor Co	Automobiles
FOXA	Twenty-First Century Fox Inc	Media
HD	Home Depot Inc. (The)	Specialty Retail
MCD	McDonald's Corp	Hotels, Restaurants & Leisure
NKE	Nike Inc	Textiles, Apparel & Luxury Goods
PCLN	Priceline.Com Inc	Internet & Catalog Retail
TWX	Time Warner Inc	Media

S&P 500 STRATEGY

INDIVIDUALLY RELEVANT FACTORS

Table 4.2 gives the individually relevant fundamental factors for the S&P 500 Consumer Discretionary segment. What is an "individually relevant" factor has been explained in the Methodology part.

Table 4.2: Individually relevant factors: S&P 500 Consumer Discretionary

FPE	Next Year Projected PE Ratio
PEG	Price/Earnings to Next Year Growth Rate
S1QG	Sales Growth Rate, Last Quarter vs. Prior Quarter (%)
POR	Payout Ratio, TTM (%)

STRATEGY DESCRIPTION

I propose a strategy using the Payout Ratio (which is individually relevant) and the Gross Margin (which is not individually relevant, but is relevant in association with other factors).

Table 4.3 provides the strategy summary.

Table 4.3: Strategy description: S&P 500 Consumer Discretionary

Name	Discretionary-SP500
Index	S&P 500
Sector	Consumer Discretionary
Rebalanced	4 weeks
Positions	10
Maximum size	10%
Rules	1- Select stocks with POR=0 2- Select 10 stocks with the highest GM
Transaction costs	0.2%

The choice of factors has been made by testing. However, I want to verify that it is a reasonable hypothesis (see my definition of quantitative investing in Part I). In other words, it can be rationalised and interpreted. Here, the interpretation is to select companies that don't pay a dividend, and have a high gross margin. They are companies more focused on growing their business than on paying shareholders an income.

It may look strange that the individually relevant factor (POR) is used only as a filter, and Gross Margin to rank companies. However simulation shows that the first rule used alone brings an additional annualised return of 3% to the reference set, and the second rule an additional annualised return under 1%. Together, they bring an additional annualised return of 5%. It means that the filter on POR is the primary source of gain.

BASIC SIMULATION

The simulation starts in January 1999. The 10 stocks selected at this time are AZO (AutoZone), BIG (Big Lots), CCMO (CC Media Holdings), CZR (Caesars Entertainment), FTLAQ (Fruit of the Loom), KSS (Kohl's Corp), KWP (King World Productions), M (Macy's), MIR (Mirage Resorts), RBK (Reebok International). Each is allotted 10% of the portfolio capital.

Note that four of them have disappeared from the stock market as publicly traded companies: FTLAQ in 2002, KWP in 1999, MIR in 2000, RBK in 2006. However they are taken into account in simulations as long as they have been a part of the S&P 500 Index at one time.

Holdings and allocations are recalculated every four weeks. In case the rebalancing date is a holiday, it is done the next trading day. The buying and selling prices are taken on market opening. As a consequence, the approximation is made that all orders are simultaneous. In this case, "all orders" means two or less: the maximum turnover is 20% and less than 10% on average. S&P 500 companies are very liquid, so it is realistic to think that orders can be filled at open price or very close to it, at least for most individual investors. For a fund with a larger money allocation by holding, techniques can be used to optimise the average cost. I do not address this subject here.

[This short explanation is given as an example to show how it works – this explanation won't be repeated for the following simulations.]

The total return is 696% (this takes into account transaction costs: about 24% for the whole period if we assume 0.1% per trade). The 61% drawdown is measured between the 2007 top and the 2008 low.

Two quick observations:

1. It would be impossible to obtain the same return by leveraging SPY: a 100% loss would be reached before the 2009 recovery.

2. The strategy recovers faster than the benchmark: it makes a new high as soon as early 2010, whereas SPY makes it in 2013.

It is said that the best fund managers have a Sharpe ratio around 0.8 on periods over a decade (in the real world, not in simulations). So, a Sharpe ratio of 0.44 is not amazing, but it is very good compared with SPY. The fact that the Sortino ratio is higher than the Sharpe ratio is also good: it shows that the deviations from the mean are stronger upward than downward. The risk (standard deviation) is higher than SPY, but it stays in the same 5% range. For a stock strategy, I consider that the correlation with the benchmark is really high above 0.7. Here, at 0.64, it is moderately high. The stock market moves are a prominent factor in the strategy performance, but not overly prominent.

Fig 4.1: Simulation data and equity curve: S&P 500 Consumer Discretionary

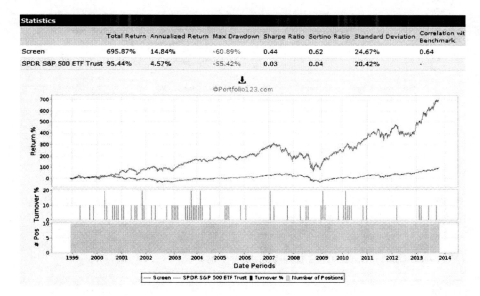

Statistics							
	Total Return	Annualized Return	Max Drawdown	Sharpe Ratio	Sortino Ratio	Standard Deviation	Correlation wit Benchmark
Screen	695.87%	14.84%	-60.89%	0.44	0.62	24.67%	0.64
SPDR S&P 500 ETF Trust	95.44%	4.57%	-55.42%	0.03	0.04	20.42%	-

NB: due to a graphical issue, there is a gap in the time axis on all charts: all simulations end on 1/1/2014.

HEDGED SIMULATION

The data and chart for the hedged simulation are obtained by combining the basic strategy with the hedging described in the previous chapter. All hedged simulations described in this book have been run on the same principle.

The return is much better than the non-hedged version, but the most impressive difference is in the max drawdown: it is divided by more than two (-61% previously, -27% here). Hedging has considerably smoothed market downturns. The Sharpe ratio is good, the Sortino ratio even better. Below 0.5, I consider that the correlation with SPY is low.

Fig 4.2: Simulation data and equity curve: S&P 500 Consumer Discretionary, Hedged

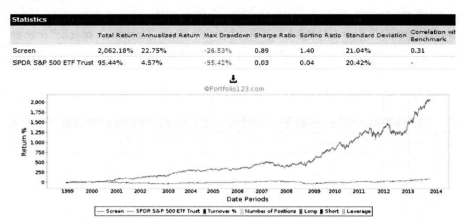

Statistics							
	Total Return	Annualized Return	Max Drawdown	Sharpe Ratio	Sortino Ratio	Standard Deviation	Correlation with Benchmark
Screen	2,062.18%	22.75%	-26.53%	0.89	1.40	21.04%	0.31
SPDR S&P 500 ETF Trust	95.44%	4.57%	-55.42%	0.03	0.04	20.42%	-

CONSISTENCY

To evaluate the consistency over time, here are the annualised returns with hedging over three, five-year periods:

Table 4.4: Consistency over five-year periods

Period	1/2/1999–1/1/2004	1/1/2004–1/1/2009	1/1/2009–1/1/2014
Annualised return	33%	9%	30%

COMMENT

Consumer Discretionary is a cyclical sector. A protection tactic is necessary to avoid heavy losses in market downturns. Hedging may be a better solution than going to cash to maximise the return and limit the drawdown. This strategy was very profitable with a greater than 30% return during the first five-year period, returns were lower but stayed profitable in the second period, then came back close to 30% in the third period.

It looks a robust strategy for the long term, but Consumer Discretionary stocks are sensitive to economic cycles. As a consequence, the return may vary significantly over shorter terms.

RUSSELL 2000 STRATEGY

INDIVIDUALLY RELEVANT FACTORS

Fundamental indicators often don't work the same way for small caps and large caps, even in the same sector. The reasons may be due to company size and specific to sectors. As a consequence, the individually relevant factors and strategies are generally found to be different.

Here are the factors from my working list that are individually relevant for the Russell 2000 Consumer Discretionary reference set:

Table 4.5: Individually relevant factors: Russell 2000 Consumer Discretionary

FPE	Next Year Projected PE Ratio
PFCF	Price To Free Cash Flow Per Share Ratio, TTM

DESCRIPTION

I propose a strategy using the two individually relevant factors in the list. A summary of this strategy is given in Table 4.6.

Table 4.6: Strategy description: Russell 2000 Consumer Discretionary

Name	Discretionary-R2000
Index	Russell 2000
Sector	Consumer Discretionary
Rebalanced	4 weeks
Positions	20
Maximum size	5%
Rules	1- select the 50 stocks with the lowest FPE
	2- select the 20 stocks with the lowest PFCF
Transaction costs	0.5%

The rationalised interpretation is to select relatively cheap companies regarding their earnings estimate and free cash flow.

Russell 2000 companies are less liquid, thus a higher figure is used to model the transaction costs.

BASIC SIMULATION

I propose an exercise for these charts in Part II: look at the numbers in the screenshots and try to interpret them the same way I did for the first reference set. You may learn much more doing it yourself than reading my interpretation. Here are the main points to look at:

- The **annualised return**. Every investor has a different idea of what is a good return. Moreover, the return alone makes little sense without looking at the max drawdown and standard deviation. For strategies using a four-week rebalancing, my opinion is that an annualised return is attractive above 20%.

- The **max drawdown**. In absolute value, each investor must determine an acceptable threshold. I consider that a max drawdown beyond -40% is scary on an individual strategy. When designing a real portfolio combining various strategies, I try to keep it below 20%, knowing that it might be worse in the future.

- The **Sharpe and Sortino ratios**. In this context I consider that below 0.5 is bad, above 0.8 is good, above 1.5 is very good.

- The **standard deviation** alone makes little sense without looking at the annualised return. However you can compare it with the benchmark's standard deviation: here 20% on the period. It gives a limit for separating relatively safe and relatively risky strategies.

- The **correlation with the benchmark** is not good or bad in itself. But as holding SPY all the time is a very risky strategy, a low correlation should be a positive clue. It is confirmed here: the best strategies in terms of risk-adjusted performance have a low correlation with SPY. Nevertheless, don't make this a rule in all contexts.

Fig 4.3: Simulation data and equity curve: Russell 2000 Consumer Discretionary

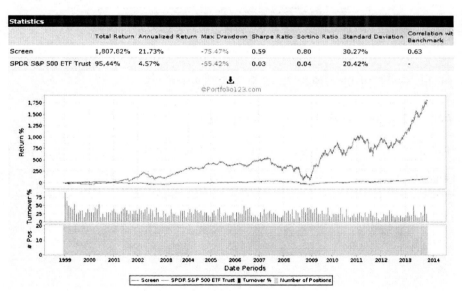

Statistics							
	Total Return	Annualized Return	Max Drawdown	Sharpe Ratio	Sortino Ratio	Standard Deviation	Correlation wit Benchmark
Screen	1,807.82%	21.73%	-75.47%	0.59	0.80	30.27%	0.63
SPDR S&P 500 ETF Trust	95.44%	4.57%	-55.42%	0.03	0.04	20.42%	-

HEDGED SIMULATION

Fig 4.4: Simulation data and equity curve: Russell 2000 Consumer Discretionary, hedged

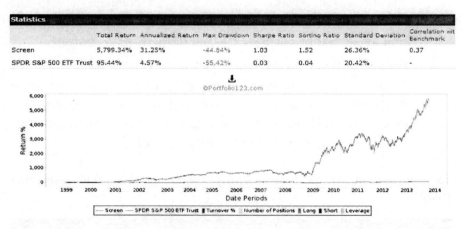

Statistics							
	Total Return	Annualized Return	Max Drawdown	Sharpe Ratio	Sortino Ratio	Standard Deviation	Correlation wit Benchmark
Screen	5,799.34%	31.25%	-44.84%	1.03	1.52	26.36%	0.37
SPDR S&P 500 ETF Trust	95.44%	4.57%	-55.42%	0.03	0.04	20.42%	-

CONSISTENCY

Annualised returns with hedging by five-year periods:

Table 4.7: Consistency over five-year periods

Period	1/2/1999–1/1/2004	1/1/2004–1/1/2009	1/1/2009–1/1/2014
Annualised Return	41%	7%	41%

COMMENT

The small cap portfolio magnifies the return and also the risk in terms of drawdown and volatility. Once again, a protection tactic is a must to avoid unacceptable drawdowns. In its hedged versions, the small cap portfolio has a slightly better risk-adjusted return (Sharp and Sortino ratios) than the large cap portfolio. The three, five-year returns show the same cyclical pattern as the S&P 500 strategy, with an even larger amplitude. Small companies are usually more volatile than large caps: they go up faster when the risk appetite leads the market, and they fall harder in a bear market.

CHAPTER 5

CONSUMER STAPLES

SECTOR OVERVIEW

DEFINITION

Here is the GICS® definition by MSCI and Standard & Poor's:

> The Consumer Staples Sector comprises companies whose businesses are less sensitive to economic cycles. It includes manufacturers and distributors of food, beverages and tobacco and producers of non-durable household goods and personal products. It also includes food & drug retailing companies as well as hypermarkets and consumer super centers.

COMPANIES

This sector contains 40 companies in the S&P 500 and 64 in the Russell 2000. Table 5.1 presents the 10 largest capitalisations at the time of writing, arranged in alphabetical order by ticker.

Table 5.1: Stock examples: S&P 500 Consumer Staples

Ticker	Name	Industry
CL	Colgate-Palmolive Co	Household Products
CVS	CVS Caremark Corp	Food & Staples Retailing
KO	Coca-Cola Co (The)	Beverages
MDLZ	Mondelez International Inc	Food Products
MO	Altria Group Inc	Tobacco
PEP	PepsiCo Inc	Beverages
PG	Procter & Gamble Co (The)	Household Products
PM	Philip Morris International Inc	Tobacco
WAG	Walgreen Co	Food & Staples Retailing
WMT	Wal-Mart Stores Inc	Food & Staples Retailing

S&P 500 STRATEGY

INDIVIDUALLY RELEVANT FACTORS

Here are the factors from my working list that are individually relevant for the
S&P 500 Consumer Staples reference set.

Table 5.2: Individually relevant factors: S&P 500 Consumer Staples

PE	Price To Earnings Ratio Including Extraordinary Items, TTM
FPE	Next Year Projected PE Ratio
S5YG	Sales Growth Rate, 5 Year (%)
ROA	Return on Assets, TTM (%)
CR	Current Ratio, Last Quarter
GM	Gross Margin, TTM (%)
NPM	Net Profit Margin, TTM (%)

STRATEGY DESCRIPTION

I propose a strategy using two factors checked as individually relevant. Table 5.3 presents the strategy description.

Table 5.3: Strategy description: S&P 500 Consumer Staples

Name	Staples-SP500
Index	S&P 500
Sector	Consumer Staples
Rebalanced	4 weeks
Positions	10
Maximum size	10%
Rules	1- Select the 20 stocks with the lower FPE 2- Select the 10 stocks with the highest NPM
Transaction costs	0.2%

The rationalised interpretation is to choose companies that are cheap relative to their earnings estimates, and with a good net profit margin.

BASIC SIMULATION

Fig 5.1: Simulation data and equity curve: S&P 500 Consumer Staples

Statistics							
	Total Return	Annualized Return	Max Drawdown	Sharpe Ratio	Sortino Ratio	Standard Deviation	Correlation with Benchmark
Screen	898.70%	16.59%	-34.34%	0.82	1.09	15.35%	0.58
SPDR S&P 500 ETF Trust	95.44%	4.57%	-55.42%	0.03	0.04	20.42%	-

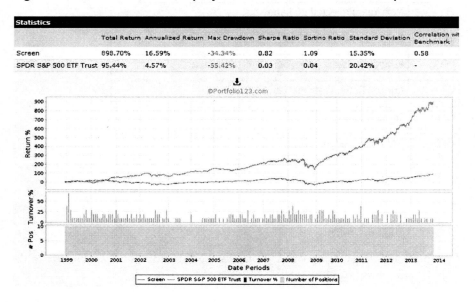

HEDGED SIMULATION

Fig 5.2: Simulation data and equity curve: S&P 500 Consumer Staples, Hedged

Statistics							
	Total Return	Annualized Return	Max Drawdown	Sharpe Ratio	Sortino Ratio	Standard Deviation	Correlation with Benchmark
Screen	2,210.17%	23.29%	-23.21%	1.28	1.87	15.04%	0.00
SPDR S&P 500 ETF Trust	95.44%	4.57%	-55.42%	0.03	0.04	20.42%	-

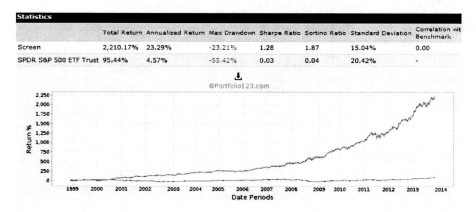

CONSISTENCY

Annualised returns with hedging by five-year periods:

Table 5.4: Consistency over five-year periods

Period	1/2/1999–1/1/2004	1/1/2004–1/1/2009	1/1/2009–1/1/2014
Annualised return	24%	18%	29%

COMMENT

Even in the basic version, the maximum drawdown and volatility look reasonable, which is a characteristic of a defensive sector. However, the hedged version gives a steadier equity curve. A Sharpe ratio above one and an even higher Sortino ratio points to a robust strategy. As explained previously, a Sortino ratio above the Sharpe ratio is a positive point: it means that the highest volatility is in gains, not losses.

The annualised return by five-year periods stays between 18% and 29%, which is remarkably stable. The sector is dominated by daily consumption products: it explains why companies are less sensitive to economic cycles.

RUSSELL 2000 STRATEGY

INDIVIDUALLY RELEVANT FACTORS

Here are the factors from my working list that are individually relevant for the Russell 2000 Consumer Staples reference set.

Table 5.5: Individually relevant factors: Russell 2000 Consumer Staples

PEG	Price/Earnings to Next Year Growth Rate
PS	Price to Sales Ratio, TTM
PFCF	Price To Free Cash Flow Per Share Ratio, TTM
ROA	Return on Assets, TTM (%)
ROE	Return on Average Common Equity, TTM (%)
NPM	Net Profit Margin, TTM (%)
POR	Payout Ratio, TTM (%)
INST	Institutional Percent Owned (%)

STRATEGY DESCRIPTION

I propose the strategy shown in Table 5.6, using two individually relevant factors.

Table 5.6: Strategy description: Russell 2000 Consumer Staples

Name	Staples-R2000
Index	Russell 2000
Sector	Consumer Staples
Rebalanced	4 weeks
Positions	20
Maximum size	5%
Rules	1- select the 50 stocks with the lowest INST
	2- select the 20 stocks with the lowest PEG
Transaction costs	0.5%

The rationalised interpretation is to select small companies that are not yet well known by institutional investors, and are cheap relative to earnings and expected growth.

BASIC SIMULATION

Fig 5.3: Simulation data and equity curve: Russell 2000 Consumer Staples

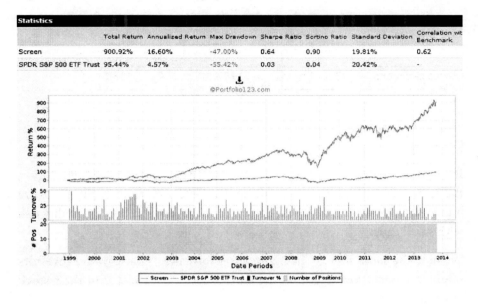

Statistics							
	Total Return	Annualized Return	Max Drawdown	Sharpe Ratio	Sortino Ratio	Standard Deviation	Correlation wit Benchmark
Screen	900.92%	16.60%	-47.00%	0.64	0.90	19.81%	0.62
SPDR S&P 500 ETF Trust	95.44%	4.57%	-55.42%	0.03	0.04	20.42%	-

HEDGED SIMULATION

Fig 5.4: Simulation data and equity curve: Russell 2000 Consumer Staples, Hedged

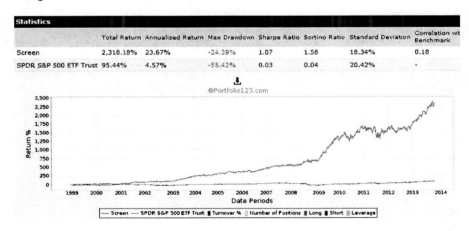

Statistics							
	Total Return	Annualized Return	Max Drawdown	Sharpe Ratio	Sortino Ratio	Standard Deviation	Correlation wit Benchmark
Screen	2,318.18%	23.67%	-24.39%	1.07	1.58	18.34%	0.18
SPDR S&P 500 ETF Trust	95.44%	4.57%	-55.42%	0.03	0.04	20.42%	-

CONSISTENCY

Annualised returns with hedging by five-year periods:

Table 5.7: Consistency over five-year periods

Period	1/2/1999–1/1/2004	1/1/2004–1/1/2009	1/1/2009–1/1/2014
Annualised return	23%	20%	28%

COMMENT

If we compare the hedged versions of the large cap and small cap portfolios, the returns and drawdowns are similar. As the Sharpe and Sortino ratios are higher with large caps, in this case there is no incentive to take a liquidity risk with small caps.

We note the same stability in five-year performance. Conservative investors might consider overweighting the Consumer Staples sector in their stock portfolio.

CHAPTER 6

ENERGY

SECTOR OVERVIEW

DEFINITION

Here is the GICS® definition by MSCI and Standard & Poor's:

> The Energy Sector comprises companies engaged in exploration & production, refining & marketing and storage & transportation of oil & gas and coal & consumable fuels. It also includes companies that offer oil & gas equipment and services.

COMPANIES

This sector contains 45 companies in the S&P 500 and 119 in the Russell 2000. Here is the list of the 10 largest capitalisations at the time of writing, arranged in alphabetical order by ticker.

Table 6.1: Stock examples: S&P 500 Energy

Ticker	Name	Industry
APC	Anadarko Petroleum Corp	Oil, Gas & Consumable Fuels
COP	ConocoPhillips	Oil, Gas & Consumable Fuels
CVX	Chevron Corp	Oil, Gas & Consumable Fuels
EOG	EOG Resources Inc.	Oil, Gas & Consumable Fuels
HAL	Halliburton Co	Energy Equipment & Services
KMI	Kinder Morgan Inc.	Oil, Gas & Consumable Fuels
OXY	Occidental Petroleum Corp	Oil, Gas & Consumable Fuels
PSX	Phillips 66	Oil, Gas & Consumable Fuels
SLB	Schlumberger Ltd	Energy Equipment & Services
XOM	Exxon Mobil Corp	Oil, Gas & Consumable Fuels

S&P 500 STRATEGY

INDIVIDUALLY RELEVANT FACTORS

Here are the factors from my working list that are individually relevant for the S&P 500 Energy reference set:

Table 6.2: Individually relevant factors: S&P 500 Energy

PB	Price to Book Ratio, Last Quarter
EPS1YG	EPS Growth Rate, TTM over prior TTM (%)
ROA	Return on Assets, TTM (%)

STRATEGY DESCRIPTION

The proposed strategy uses a single valuation ratio, as shown along with the other strategy specifics in Table 6.3.

Table 6.3: Strategy description: S&P 500 Energy

Name	Energy-SP500
Index	S&P 500
Sector	Energy
Rebalanced	4 weeks
Positions	10
Maximum size	10%
Rules	Select the 10 stocks with the lowest PB
Transaction costs	0.2%

The rationalised interpretation is to select stocks that are cheap relative to the company's accounting value.

BASIC SIMULATION

Fig 6.1: Simulation data and equity curve: S&P 500 Energy

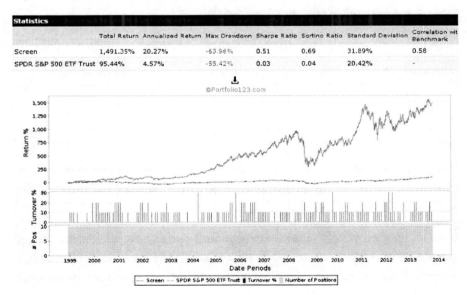

Statistics							
	Total Return	Annualized Return	Max Drawdown	Sharpe Ratio	Sortino Ratio	Standard Deviation	Correlation with Benchmark
Screen	1,491.35%	20.27%	-63.96%	0.51	0.69	31.89%	0.58
SPDR S&P 500 ETF Trust	95.44%	4.57%	-55.42%	0.03	0.04	20.42%	-

HEDGED SIMULATION

Fig 6.2: Simulation data and equity curve: S&P 500 Energy, Hedged

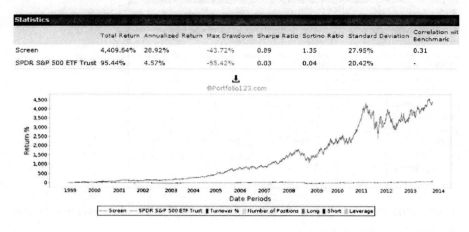

Statistics	Total Return	Annualized Return	Max Drawdown	Sharpe Ratio	Sortino Ratio	Standard Deviation	Correlation wit Benchmark
Screen	4,409.64%	28.92%	-43.72%	0.89	1.35	27.95%	0.31
SPDR S&P 500 ETF Trust	95.44%	4.57%	-55.42%	0.03	0.04	20.42%	-

CONSISTENCY

Annualised returns with hedging by five-year periods:

Table 6.4: Consistency over five-year periods

Period	1/2/1999–1/1/2004	1/1/2004–1/1/2009	1/1/2009–1/1/2014
Annualised return	29%	31%	26%

COMMENT

Drawdowns and standard deviations are those of a cyclical sector. A protection tactic is necessary. The annualised return is better than for Consumer Staples, but the risk-adjusted return is lower.

It is a sector theoretically sensitive to economic cycles, nevertheless the hedged version shows an impressive stability for annualised returns in the three, five-year periods. In fact, it hides big differences from one year to another, especially since 2009: 2011 was a very bad year with a large drawdown and a negative annual return.

RUSSELL 2000 STRATEGY

INDIVIDUALLY RELEVANT FACTORS

Here are the factors from my working list that are individually relevant for the Russell 2000 Energy reference set:

Table 6.5: Individually relevant factors: Russell 2000 Energy

FPE	Next Year Projected PE Ratio
PS	Price to Sales Ratio, TTM
ROA	Return on Assets, TTM (%)
ROE	Return on Average Common Equity, TTM (%)
CR	Current Ratio, Last Quarter
POR	Payout Ratio, TTM (%)
INST	Institutional Percent Owned (%)

STRATEGY DESCRIPTION

The strategy uses two factors based on dividend and valuation.

Table 6.6: Strategy description: Russell 2000 Energy

Name	Energy-R2000
Index	Russell 2000
Sector	Energy
Rebalanced	4 weeks
Positions	20
Maximum size	5%
Rules	1- select the 50 stocks with the highest POR
	2- select the 20 stocks with the lowest PS
Transaction costs	0.5%

The rationalised interpretation is to select companies that are focused on shareholders' income, and that are cheap relative to sales. This is quite typical of energy infrastructure companies.

BASIC SIMULATION

Fig 6.3: Simulation data and equity curve: Russell 2000 Energy

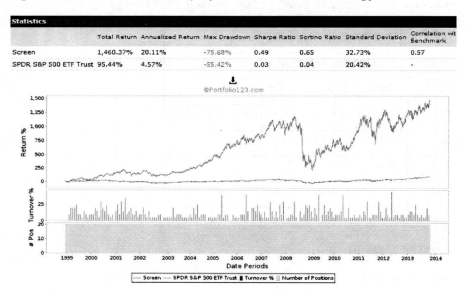

Statistics	Total Return	Annualized Return	Max Drawdown	Sharpe Ratio	Sortino Ratio	Standard Deviation	Correlation with Benchmark
Screen	1,460.37%	20.11%	-75.68%	0.49	0.65	32.73%	0.57
SPDR S&P 500 ETF Trust	95.44%	4.57%	-55.42%	0.03	0.04	20.42%	-

HEDGED SIMULATION

Fig 6.4: Simulation data and equity curve: Russell 2000 Energy, Hedged

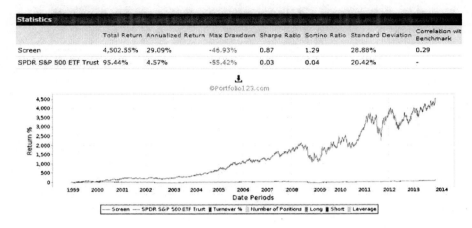

Statistics	Total Return	Annualized Return	Max Drawdown	Sharpe Ratio	Sortino Ratio	Standard Deviation	Correlation wit Benchmark
Screen	4,502.55%	29.09%	-46.93%	0.87	1.29	28.88%	0.29
SPDR S&P 500 ETF Trust	95.44%	4.57%	-55.42%	0.03	0.04	20.42%	-

CONSISTENCY

Annualised returns with hedging by five-year periods:

Table 6.7: Consistency over five-year periods

Period	1/2/1999–1/1/2004	1/1/2004–1/1/2009	1/1/2009–1/1/2014
Annualised Return	35%	24%	30%

COMMENT

The characteristics in return and risk are not better than for the large cap strategy in the same sector. Taking a liquidity risk with small caps is not justified here. The pattern by period is the same as for large cap energy stocks: a remarkably stable annualised return for the five-year periods, with large drawdowns along the road.

CHAPTER 7

FINANCIALS

SECTOR OVERVIEW

DEFINITION

Here is the GICS® definition by MSCI and Standard & Poor's:

> The Financials Sector contains companies involved in banking, thrifts & mortgage finance, specialized finance, consumer finance, asset management and custody banks, investment banking and brokerage and insurance. This Sector also includes real estate companies and REITs.

COMPANIES

This sector contains 81 companies in the S&P 500 and 478 in the Russell 2000, making it the largest for small caps. Here is the list of the 10 largest capitalisations at the time of writing, arranged in alphabetical order by ticker:

Table 7.1: Stock examples: S&P 500 Financials

Ticker	Name	Industry
AIG	American International Group Inc	Insurance
AXP	American Express Co	Consumer Finance
BAC	Bank of America Corp	Diversified Financial Services
BRK.B	Berkshire Hathaway Inc	Diversified Financial Services
C	Citigroup Inc	Diversified Financial Services
GS	Goldman Sachs Group Inc (The)	Capital Markets
JPM	JPMorgan Chase & Co	Diversified Financial Services
MS	Morgan Stanley	Capital Markets
USB	U.S. Bancorp	Commercial Banks
WFC	Wells Fargo & Co	Commercial Banks

S&P 500 STRATEGY

INDIVIDUALLY RELEVANT FACTORS

Here are the factors from my working list that are individually relevant for the S&P 500 Financials reference set:

Table 7.2: Individually relevant factors: S&P 500 Financials

PE	Price To Earnings Ratio Including Extraordinary Items, TTM
FPE	Next Year Projected PE Ratio
PS	Price to Sales Ratio, TTM
PB	Price to Book Ratio, Last Quarter
ROA	Return on Assets, TTM (%)

STRATEGY DESCRIPTION

I propose a strategy using only the most famous valuation ratio: price to earnings.

Table 7.3: Strategy description: S&P 500 Financials

Name	Financials-SP500
Index	S&P 500
Sector	Financials
Rebalanced	4 weeks
Positions	10
Maximum size	10%
Rules	Select the 10 stocks with the lowest PE
Transaction costs	0.2%

This rule selects the cheapest companies relative to their earnings.

BASIC SIMULATION

Fig 7.1: Simulation data and equity curve: S&P 500 Financials

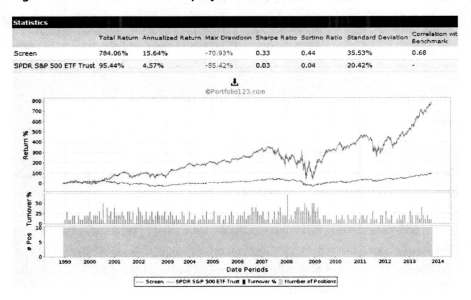

Statistics		Total Return	Annualized Return	Max Drawdown	Sharpe Ratio	Sortino Ratio	Standard Deviation	Correlation with Benchmark
Screen		784.06%	15.64%	-70.93%	0.33	0.44	35.53%	0.68
SPDR S&P 500 ETF Trust	95.44%	4.57%	-55.42%	0.03	0.04	20.42%	-

HEDGED SIMULATION

Fig 7.2: Simulation data and equity curve: S&P 500 Financials, Hedged

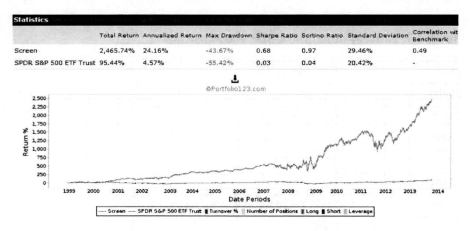

Statistics							
	Total Return	Annualized Return	Max Drawdown	Sharpe Ratio	Sortino Ratio	Standard Deviation	Correlation wit Benchmark
Screen	2,465.74%	24.16%	-43.67%	0.68	0.97	29.46%	0.49
SPDR S&P 500 ETF Trust	95.44%	4.57%	-55.42%	0.03	0.04	20.42%	-

CONSISTENCY

Annualised returns with hedging by five-year periods:

Table 7.4: Consistency over five-year periods

Period	1/2/1999–1/1/2004	1/1/2004–1/1/2009	1/1/2009–1/1/2014
Annualised return	32%	15%	27%

COMMENT

Financial stocks are volatile in market downturns. Even in its hedged version, the portfolio shows deep drawdowns. The five-year annualised returns remain high, with a dip in the middle period due to the 2008 financial crisis. But on a yearly basis, 2011 was worse than 2008 for the hedged version. Hedging was triggered by the timing indicators in 2008, not in 2011. When this happens, a 20% market correction may be more harmful than a 50% crash. Both the first and the last periods are above 25%, which can be considered indicative of the robustness over the long term.

RUSSELL 2000 STRATEGY

INDIVIDUALLY RELEVANT FACTORS

Here are the factors from my working list that are individually relevant for the Russell 2000 Financials reference set:

Table 7.5: Individually relevant factors: Russell 2000 Financials

PB	Price to Book Ratio, Last Quarter
S5YG	Sales Growth Rate, 5 Year (%)
ROA	Return on Assets, TTM (%)
ROE	Return on Average Common Equity, TTM (%)

STRATEGY DESCRIPTION

I propose a strategy using a single profitability ratio.

Table 7.6: Strategy description: Russell 2000 Financials

Name	Financials-R2000
Index	Russell 2000
Sector	Financials
Rebalanced	4 weeks
Positions	20
Maximum size	5%
Rules	Select the 20 stocks with the highest ROA
Transaction costs	0.5%

The rationalised interpretation is to pick the most profitable companies relative to their assets.

BASIC SIMULATION

Fig 7.3: Simulation data and equity curve: Russell 2000 Financials

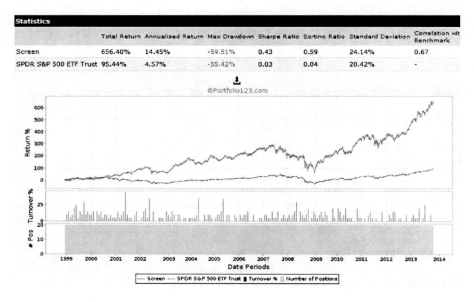

Statistics							
	Total Return	Annualized Return	Max Drawdown	Sharpe Ratio	Sortino Ratio	Standard Deviation	Correlation wit Benchmark
Screen	656.40%	14.45%	-59.51%	0.43	0.59	24.14%	0.67
SPDR S&P 500 ETF Trust	95.44%	4.57%	-55.42%	0.03	0.04	20.42%	-

HEDGED SIMULATION

Fig 7.4: Simulation data and equity curve: Russell 2000 Financials, Hedged

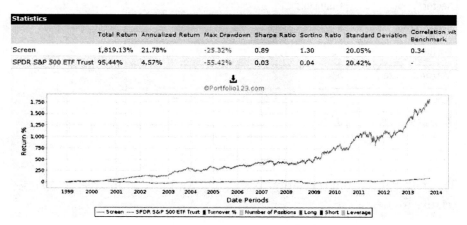

Statistics							
	Total Return	Annualized Return	Max Drawdown	Sharpe Ratio	Sortino Ratio	Standard Deviation	Correlation wit Benchmark
Screen	1,819.13%	21.78%	-25.32%	0.89	1.30	20.05%	0.34
SPDR S&P 500 ETF Trust	95.44%	4.57%	-55.42%	0.03	0.04	20.42%	-

CONSISTENCY

Annualised returns with hedging by five-year periods:

Table 7.7: Consistency over five-year periods

Period	1/2/1999–1/1/2004	1/1/2004–1/1/2009	1/1/2009–1/1/2014
Annualised return	37%	9%	27%

COMMENT

In Financials, it seems that smaller is safer. The small cap portfolio has a lower risk in drawdown and volatility, and has a better risk-adjusted performance measured by the Sortino ratio. The five-year returns pattern is different from large caps: the return is much lower in the middle period. However, it recovers in the last period.

CHAPTER 8

HEALTH CARE

SECTOR OVERVIEW

DEFINITION

Here is the GICS® definition by MSCI and Standard & Poor's:

> The Health Care Sector includes health care providers & services, companies that manufacture and distribute health care equipments & supplies and health care technology companies. It also includes companies involved in the research, development, production and marketing of pharmaceuticals and biotechnology products.

COMPANIES

This sector contains 54 companies in the S&P 500 and 256 in the Russell 2000. Here is the list of the 10 largest capitalisations at the time of writing, arranged in alphabetical order by ticker:

Table 8.1: Stock examples: S&P 500 Health Care

Ticker	Name	Industry
ABBV	AbbVie Inc	Pharmaceuticals
AMGN	Amgen Inc.	Biotechnology
BIIB	Biogen Idec Inc	Biotechnology
BMY	Bristol-Myers Squibb Co	Pharmaceuticals
CELG	Celgene Corp	Biotechnology
GILD	Gilead Sciences Inc	Biotechnology
JNJ	Johnson & Johnson	Pharmaceuticals
MRK	Merck & Co Inc.	Pharmaceuticals
PFE	Pfizer Inc	Pharmaceuticals
UNH	Unitedhealth Group Inc	Health Care Providers & Services

S&P 500 STRATEGY

INDIVIDUALLY RELEVANT FACTORS

Here are the factors from my working list that are individually relevant for the S&P 500 Health Care reference set.

Table 8.2: Individually relevant factors: S&P 500 Health Care

PE	Price To Earnings Ratio Including Extraordinary Items, TTM
FPE	Next Year Projected PE Ratio
PS	Price to Sales Ratio, TTM
PB	Price to Book Ratio, Last Quarter
PFCF	Price To Free Cash Flow Per Share Ratio, TTM
S5YG	Sales Growth Rate, 5 Year (%)
ROA	Return on Assets, TTM (%)
CR	Current Ratio, Last Quarter
GM	Gross Margin, TTM (%)
NPM	Net Profit Margin, TTM (%)
POR	Payout Ratio, TTM (%)

STRATEGY DESCRIPTION

This strategy uses a single valuation ratio.

Table 8.3: Strategy description: S&P 500 Health Care

Name	Healthcare-SP500
Index	S&P 500
Sector	Health Care
Rebalanced	4 weeks
Positions	10
Maximum size	10%
Rules	Select the 10 stocks with the lowest FPE
Transaction costs	0.2%

The rationalised interpretation is to select cheap stocks relative to the next year's earnings estimate.

BASIC SIMULATION

Fig 8.1: Simulation data and equity curve: S&P 500 Health Care

Statistics	Total Return	Annualized Return	Max Drawdown	Sharpe Ratio	Sortino Ratio	Standard Deviation	Correlation with Benchmark
Screen	1,147.93%	18.33%	-56.43%	0.63	0.86	22.70%	0.54
SPDR S&P 500 ETF Trust	95.44%	4.57%	-55.42%	0.03	0.04	20.42%	-

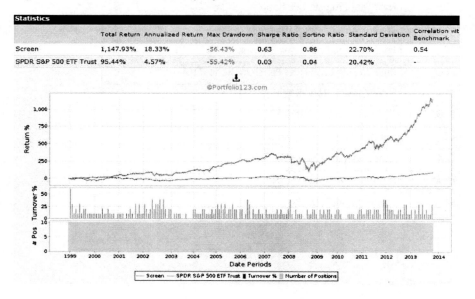

HEDGED SIMULATION

Fig 8.2: Simulation data and equity curve: S&P 500 Health Care, Hedged

Statistics	Total Return	Annualized Return	Max Drawdown	Sharpe Ratio	Sortino Ratio	Standard Deviation	Correlation with Benchmark
Screen	2,966.33%	25.64%	-33.24%	1.07	1.51	20.29%	0.15
SPDR S&P 500 ETF Trust	95.44%	4.57%	-55.42%	0.03	0.04	20.42%	-

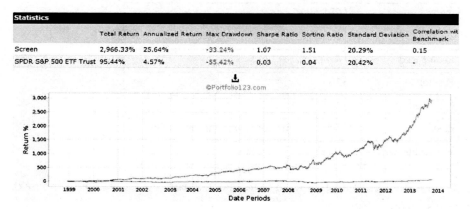

CONSISTENCY

Annualised returns with hedging by five-year periods:

Table 8.4: Consistency over five-year periods

Period	1/2/1999–1/1/2004	1/1/2004–1/1/2009	1/1/2009–1/1/2014
Annualised return	26%	19%	35%

COMMENT

With a Sharpe ratio above 1 and a Sortino ratio above 1.5, the hedged Health care-SP500 portfolio looks very robust. Annualised returns on five-year periods are very steady, with a surge since 2009. It may be explained by two demographic factors:

1. an aging population and the baby-boom generation boosts the consumption of health care products and services in developed countries, and

2. the fast growth of a global middle class has the same effect in developing countries.

These phenomena should continue to lift the sector in the next decade, with possible bubbles on the way, especially in the biotechnology industry.

RUSSELL 2000 STRATEGY

INDIVIDUALLY RELEVANT FACTORS

Here are the factors from my working list that are individually relevant for the Russell 2000 Health Care reference set:

Table 8.5: Individually relevant factors: Russell 2000 Health Care

PE	Price To Earnings Ratio Including Extraordinary Items, TTM
FPE	Next Year Projected PE Ratio
PS	Price to Sales Ratio, TTM
PB	Price to Book Ratio, Last Quarter
PFCF	Price To Free Cash Flow Per Share Ratio, TTM
EPS1YG	EPS Growth Rate, TTM over prior TTM (%)
ROA	Return on Assets, TTM (%)
ROE	Return on Average Common Equity, TTM (%)
GM	Gross Margin, TTM (%)
NPM	Net Profit Margin, TTM (%)
POR	Payout Ratio, TTM (%)

STRATEGY DESCRIPTION

I propose to use a single valuation ratio in this strategy.

Table 8.6: Strategy description: Russell 2000 Health Care

Name	Healthcare-R2000
Index	Russell 2000
Sector	Health Care
Rebalanced	4 weeks
Positions	20
Maximum size	5%
Rules	Select the 20 companies with the lowest PS
Transaction costs	0.5%

Rationalised interpretation: this strategy selects cheap companies relative to sales. Because of the reference to sales, it excludes de facto young companies that are in a pure research and development stage. It prefers companies with an existing flow of products and services.

BASIC SIMULATION

Fig 8.3: Simulation data and equity curve: Russell 2000 Health Care

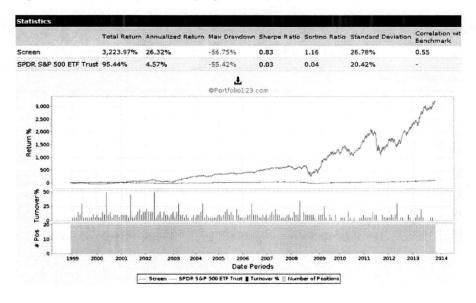

Statistics	Total Return	Annualized Return	Max Drawdown	Sharpe Ratio	Sortino Ratio	Standard Deviation	Correlation wit Benchmark
Screen	3,223.97%	26.32%	-56.75%	0.83	1.16	26.78%	0.55
SPDR S&P 500 ETF Trust	95.44%	4.57%	-55.42%	0.03	0.04	20.42%	-

HEDGED SIMULATION

Fig 8.4: Simulation data and equity curve: Russell 2000 Health Care, Hedged

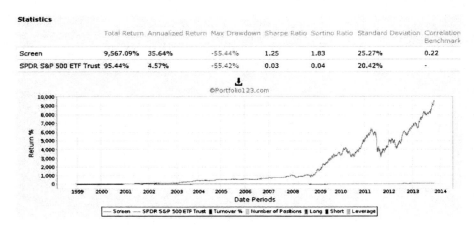

Statistics	Total Return	Annualized Return	Max Drawdown	Sharpe Ratio	Sortino Ratio	Standard Deviation	Correlation Benchmark
Screen	9,567.09%	35.64%	-55.44%	1.25	1.83	25.27%	0.22
SPDR S&P 500 ETF Trust	95.44%	4.57%	-55.42%	0.03	0.04	20.42%	-

CONSISTENCY

Annualised returns with hedging by five-year periods:

Table 8.7: Consistency over five-year periods

Period	1/2/1999–1/1/2004	1/1/2004–1/1/2009	1/1/2009–1/1/2014
Annualised return	38%	23%	46%

COMMENT

The annualised return and risk-adjusted performance are better than for the large cap strategy, at the price of a higher maximum drawdown. The five-year returns pattern is similar to large caps and amplifies the strength of the trend over the last five years – showing an impressive 46% annualised return.

CHAPTER 9

INDUSTRIALS

SECTOR OVERVIEW

DEFINITION

Here is the GICS® definition by MSCI and Standard & Poor's:

> The Industrials Sector includes manufacturers and distributors of capital goods such as aerospace & defense, building products, electrical equipment and machinery and companies that offer construction & engineering services. It also includes providers of commercial & professional services including printing, environmental and facilities services, office services & supplies, security & alarm services, human resource & employment services, research & consulting services. It also includes companies that provide transportation services.

COMPANIES

This sector contains 64 companies in the S&P 500 and 251 in the Russell 2000. Here is the list of the 10 largest capitalisations at the time of writing, arranged in alphabetical order by ticker:

Table 9.1: Stock examples: S&P 500 Industrials

Ticker	Name	Industry
BA	Boeing Co (The)	Aerospace & Defense
CAT	Caterpillar Inc	Machinery
DHR	Danaher Corp	Industrial Conglomerates
GE	General Electric Co	Industrial Conglomerates
HON	Honeywell International Inc.	Aerospace & Defense
LMT	Lockheed Martin Corp	Aerospace & Defense
MMM	3M Co	Industrial Conglomerates
UNP	Union Pacific Corp	Road & Rail
UPS	United Parcel Service Inc	Air Freight & Logistics
UTX	United Technologies Corp	Aerospace & Defense

S&P 500 STRATEGY

INDIVIDUALLY RELEVANT FACTORS

Here are the factors from my working list that are individually relevant for the S&P 500 Industrials reference set:

Table 9.2: Individually relevant factors: S&P 500 Industrials

PE	Price To Earnings Ratio Including Extraordinary Items, TTM
PB	Price to Book Ratio, Last Quarter

STRATEGY DESCRIPTION

This strategy uses a single valuation ratio.

Table 9.3: Strategy description: S&P 500 Industrials

Name	Industrials-SP500
Index	S&P 500
Sector	Industrials
Rebalanced	4 weeks
Positions	10
Maximum size	10%
Rules	Select the 10 stocks with the lowest PE
Transaction costs	0.2%

The rationalised interpretation is to select companies that are cheap relative to their earnings.

BASIC SIMULATION

Fig 9.1: Simulation data and equity curve: S&P 500 Industrials

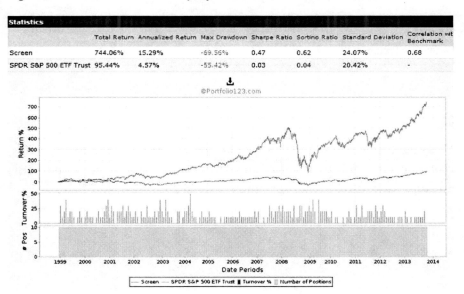

Statistics	Total Return	Annualized Return	Max Drawdown	Sharpe Ratio	Sortino Ratio	Standard Deviation	Correlation wit Benchmark
Screen	744.06%	15.29%	-69.56%	0.47	0.62	24.07%	0.68
SPDR S&P 500 ETF Trust	95.44%	4.57%	-55.42%	0.03	0.04	20.42%	-

HEDGED SIMULATION

Fig 9.2: Simulation data and equity curve: S&P 500 Industrials, Hedged

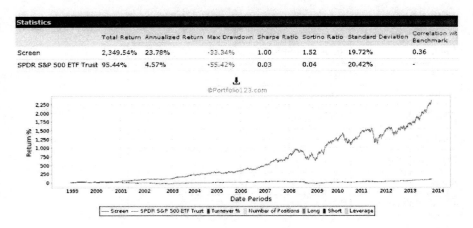

Statistics	Total Return	Annualized Return	Max Drawdown	Sharpe Ratio	Sortino Ratio	Standard Deviation	Correlation wit Benchmark
Screen	2,349.54%	23.78%	-33.34%	1.00	1.52	19.72%	0.36
SPDR S&P 500 ETF Trust	95.44%	4.57%	-55.42%	0.03	0.04	20.42%	-

©Portfolio123.com

CONSISTENCY

Annualised returns with hedging by five-year periods:

Table 9.4: Consistency over five-year periods

Period	1/2/1999–1/1/2004	1/1/2004–1/1/2009	1/1/2009–1/1/2014
Annualised return	26%	23%	25%

COMMENT

Hedging brings to Industrials-SP500 good Sharpe and Sortino ratios, especially for a strategy in a cyclical sector. The five-year annualised returns are impressively stable, hiding a bumpy ride in 2008, 2010 and 2011.

RUSSELL 2000 STRATEGY

INDIVIDUALLY RELEVANT FACTORS

Here are the factors from my working list that are individually relevant for the Russell 2000 Industrials reference set:

Table 9.5: Individually relevant factors: Russell 2000 Industrials

PE	Price To Earnings Ratio Including Extraordinary Items, TTM
FPE	Next Year Projected PE Ratio
PEG	Price/Earnings to Next Year Growth Rate
PS	Price to Sales Ratio, TTM
PB	Price to Book Ratio, Last Quarter
PFCF	Price To Free Cash Flow Per Share Ratio, TTM
EPS1YG	EPS Growth Rate, TTM over prior TTM (%)
S5YG	Sales Growth Rate, 5 Year (%)
GM	Gross Margin, TTM (%)

STRATEGY DESCRIPTION

The next strategy uses two valuation ratios. The strategy description is shown in Table 9.6.

The rationalised interpretation is to select companies that are cheap relative to their sales and free cash flow.

The Lazy Fundamental Analyst | Fred Piard

Table 9.6: Strategy description: Russell 2000 Industrials

Name	Industrials-R2000
Index	Russell 2000
Sector	Industrials
Rebalanced	4 weeks
Positions	20
Maximum size	5%
Rules	1-select the 50 stocks with the lowest PS
	2-select the 20 stocks with the lowest PFCF
Transaction costs	0.5%

BASIC SIMULATION

Fig 9.3: Simulation data and equity curve: Russell 2000 Industrials

Statistics

	Total Return	Annualized Return	Max Drawdown	Sharpe Ratio	Sortino Ratio	Standard Deviation	Correlation Benchmark
Screen	2,203.31%	23.27%	-77.66%	0.58	0.80	33.16%	0.62
SPDR S&P 500 ETF Trust	95.44%	4.57%	-55.42%	0.03	0.04	20.42%	-

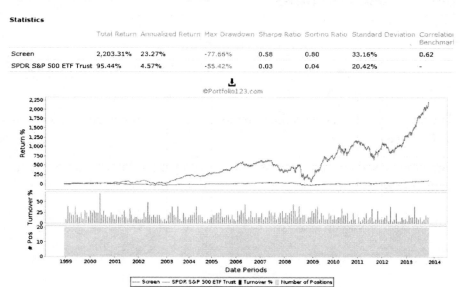

©Portfolio123.com

82

HEDGED SIMULATION

Fig 9.4: Simulation data and equity curve: Russell 2000 Industrials

Statistics

	Total Return	Annualized Return	Max Drawdown	Sharpe Ratio	Sortino Ratio	Standard Deviation	Correlation Benchmark
Screen	7,105.93%	33.01%	-43.67%	1.02	1.55	28.40%	0.39
SPDR S&P 500 ETF Trust	95.44%	4.57%	-55.42%	0.03	0.04	20.42%	-

©Portfolio123.com

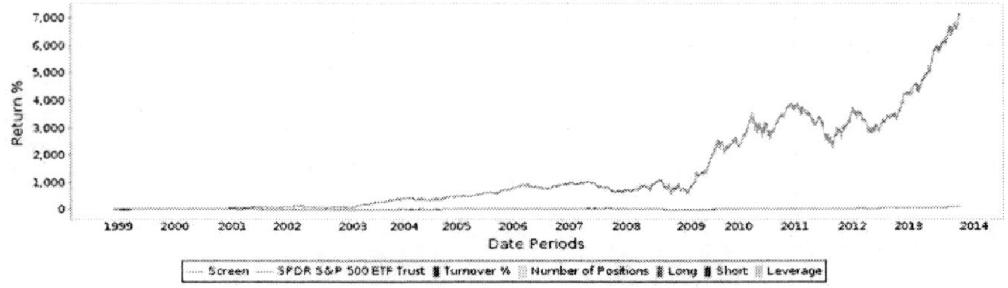

CONSISTENCY

Annualised returns with hedging by five-year periods:

Table 9.7: Consistency over five-year periods

Period	1/2/1999–1/1/2004	1/1/2004–1/1/2009	1/1/2009–1/1/2014
Annualised return	33%	20%	53%

COMMENT

In Industrials, the small cap strategy gives a significantly better performance than the large caps. It may be worth taking the additional liquidity risk for this better performance. All five-year annualised returns are above 20%, with a surge above 50% on the last period.

CHAPTER 10

INFORMATION TECHNOLOGY

SECTOR OVERVIEW

DEFINITION

H ere is the GICS® definition by MSCI and Standard & Poor's:

> The Information Technology Sector comprises companies that offer software and information technology services, manufacturers and distributors of technology hardware & equipment such as communications equipment, cellular phones, computers & peripherals, electronic equipment and related instruments and semiconductors.

COMPANIES

This sector contains 65 companies in the S&P 500 and 321 in the Russell 2000. Here is the list of the 10 largest capitalisations at the time of writing, arranged in alphabetical order by ticker:

Table 10.1: Stock examples: S&P 500 Information Technology

Ticker	Name	Industry
AAPL	Apple Inc	Computers & Peripherals
CSCO	Cisco Systems Inc	Communications Equipment
FB	Facebook Inc	Internet Software & Services
GOOG	Google Inc	Internet Software & Services
IBM	International Business Machines Corp	IT Services
INTC	Intel Corp	Semiconductors & Semiconductor Equipment
MSFT	Microsoft Corp	Software
ORCL	Oracle Corp	Software
QCOM	QUALCOMM Inc.	Communications Equipment
V	Visa Inc	IT Services

S&P 500 STRATEGY

INDIVIDUALLY RELEVANT FACTORS

Here are the factors from my working list that are individually relevant for the S&P 500 Information Technology reference set:

Table 10.2: Individually relevant factors: S&P 500 Information Technology

PEG	Price/Earnings to Next Year Growth Rate
PB	Price to Book Ratio, Last Quarter
PFCF	Price To Free Cash Flow Per Share Ratio, TTM
S5YG	Sales Growth Rate, 5 Year (%)
S1QG	Sales Growth Rate, Last Quarter vs. Prior Quarter (%)
ROA	Return on Assets, TTM (%)
INST	Institutional Percent Owned (%)

STRATEGY DESCRIPTION

I will use two valuation ratios. One is individually relevant, the other is not.

Table 10.3: Strategy description: S&P 500 Information Technology

Name	Tech-SP500
Index	S&P 500
Sector	Information Technology
Rebalanced	4 weeks
Positions	10
Maximum size	10%
Rules	1-select the 20 stocks with the lowest PB
	2-select the 10 stocks with the lowest PE
Transaction costs	0.2%

Rationalised interpretation: this strategy selects companies that are cheap regarding first their accounting value and second their earnings.

BASIC SIMULATION

Fig 10.1: Simulation data and equity curve: S&P 500 Information Technology

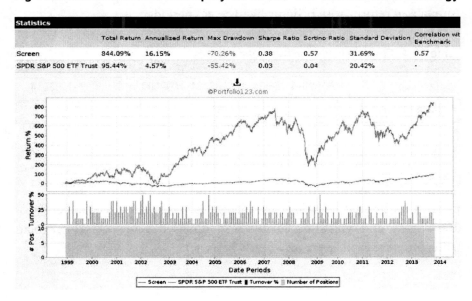

Statistics							
	Total Return	Annualized Return	Max Drawdown	Sharpe Ratio	Sortino Ratio	Standard Deviation	Correlation with Benchmark
Screen	844.09%	16.15%	-70.26%	0.38	0.57	31.69%	0.57
SPDR S&P 500 ETF Trust	95.44%	4.57%	-55.42%	0.03	0.04	20.42%	-

HEDGED SIMULATION

Fig 10.2: Simulation data and equity curve: S&P 500 Information Technology, Hedged

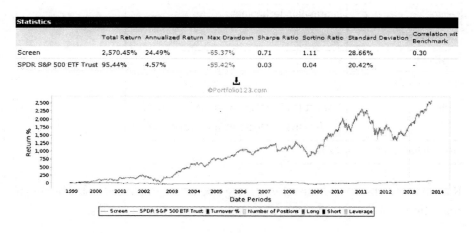

Statistics							
	Total Return	Annualized Return	Max Drawdown	Sharpe Ratio	Sortino Ratio	Standard Deviation	Correlation wit Benchmark
Screen	2,570.45%	24.49%	-65.37%	0.71	1.11	28.66%	0.30
SPDR S&P 500 ETF Trust	95.44%	4.57%	-55.42%	0.03	0.04	20.42%	-

CONSISTENCY

Annualised returns with hedging by five-year periods:

Table 10.4: Consistency over five-year periods

Period	1/2/1999–1/1/2004	1/1/2004–1/1/2009	1/1/2009–1/1/2014
Annualised return	44%	10%	22%

COMMENT

Even in its hedged version, this strategy incurs a high risk in terms of drawdowns and volatility. Five-year annualised returns are irregular. Differences are even larger on a yearly basis.

RUSSELL 2000 STRATEGY

Here are the factors from my working list that are individually relevant for the Russell 2000 Information Technology reference set:

Table 10.5: Individually relevant factors: Russell 2000 Information Technology

FPE	Next Year Projected PE Ratio
PS	Price to Sales Ratio, TTM
PFCF	Price To Free Cash Flow Per Share Ratio, TTM
ROA	Return on Assets, TTM (%)
ROE	Return on Average Common Equity, TTM (%)
GM	Gross Margin, TTM (%)
NPM	Net Profit Margin, TTM (%)
INST	Institutional Percent Owned (%)

STRATEGY DESCRIPTION

I will use a factor on profitability and another one on valuation.

Table 10.6: Strategy description: Russell 2000 Information Technology

Name	Tech-R2000
Index	Russell 2000
Sector	Information Technology
Rebalanced	4 weeks
Positions	20
Maximum size	5%
Rules	1- select the 100 stocks with the highest GM
	2- select the 20 stocks with the lowest PFCF
Transaction costs	0.5%

Rationalised interpretation: this strategy selects companies that are cheap relative to their cash flow, among those that have the best gross margin. Because of the reference to margin and cash flow, it excludes pure development-stage companies. In the following simulation, you can see that it would have resisted very well the dot-com crash (2000–2002) by avoiding weak business models. It should also help in case history repeats itself.

BASIC SIMULATION

Fig 10.3: Simulation data and equity curve: Russell 2000 Information Technology

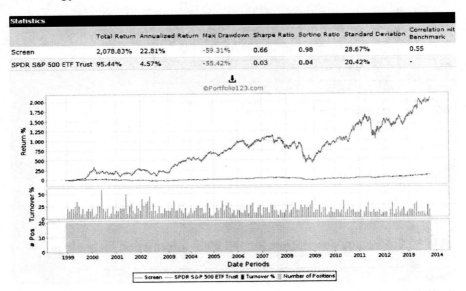

Statistics							
	Total Return	Annualized Return	Max Drawdown	Sharpe Ratio	Sortino Ratio	Standard Deviation	Correlation wit Benchmark
Screen	2,078.83%	22.81%	-59.31%	0.66	0.98	28.67%	0.55
SPDR S&P 500 ETF Trust	95.44%	4.57%	-55.42%	0.03	0.04	20.42%	-

HEDGED SIMULATION

Fig 10.4: Simulation data and equity curve: Russell 2000 Information Technology, Hedged

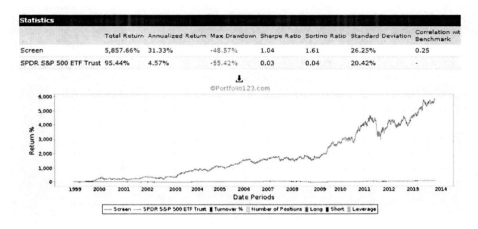

Statistics	Total Return	Annualized Return	Max Drawdown	Sharpe Ratio	Sortino Ratio	Standard Deviation	Correlation wit Benchmark
Screen	5,857.66%	31.33%	-48.57%	1.04	1.61	26.25%	0.25
SPDR S&P 500 ETF Trust	95.44%	4.57%	-55.42%	0.03	0.04	20.42%	-

©Portfolio123.com

CONSISTENCY

Annualised returns with hedging by five-year periods:

Table 10.7: Consistency over five-year periods

Period	1/2/1999–1/1/2004	1/1/2004–1/1/2009	1/1/2009–1/1/2014
Annualised return	60%	14%	30%

COMMENT

Like Financials, in the IT sector small is beautiful. The Russell 2000 portfolio is safer and more rewarding than the S&P 500 portfolio. Like for large caps, it is very irregular in annualised return.

CHAPTER 11

MATERIALS

SECTOR OVERVIEW

DEFINITION

Here is the GICS® definition by MSCI and Standard & Poor's:

> The Materials Sector includes companies that manufacture chemicals, construction materials, glass, paper, forest products and related packaging products, and metals, minerals and mining companies, including producers of steel.

COMPANIES

This sector contains 31 companies in the S&P 500 and 87 in the Russell 2000. Here is the list of the 10 largest capitalisations at the time of writing, arranged in alphabetical order by ticker:

Table 11.1: Stock examples: S&P 500 Materials

Ticker	Name	Industry
APD	Air Products and Chemicals Inc.	Chemicals
DD	E. I. du Pont de Nemours and Co	Chemicals
DOW	Dow Chemical Co (The)	Chemicals
ECL	Ecolab Inc.	Chemicals
FCX	Freeport-McMoran Copper & Gold Inc.	Metals & Mining
IP	International Paper Co	Paper & Forest Products
LYB	LyondellBasell Industries NV	Chemicals
MON	Monsanto Co	Chemicals
PPG	PPG Industries Inc.	Chemicals
PX	Praxair Inc.	Chemicals

S&P 500 STRATEGY

INDIVIDUALLY RELEVANT FACTORS

Here are the factors from my working list that are individually relevant for the S&P 500 Materials reference set:

Table 11.2: Individually relevant factors

PFCF	Price To Free Cash Flow Per Share Ratio, TTM
EPS1YG	EPS Growth Rate, TTM over prior TTM (%)

STRATEGY DESCRIPTION

I will use only a valuation ratio here.

The rationalised interpretation is to select cheap companies relative to the free cash flow.

Table 11.3: Strategy description: S&P 500 Materials

Name	Materials-SP500
Index	S&P 500
Sector	Materials
Rebalanced	4 weeks
Positions	10
Maximum size	10%
Rules	Select the 10 stocks with the lowest PFCF
Transaction costs	0.2%

BASIC SIMULATION

Fig 11.1: Simulation data and equity curve: S&P 500 Materials

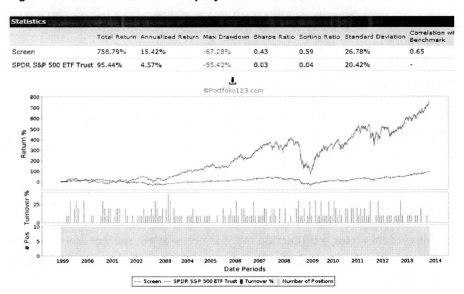

Statistics							
	Total Return	Annualized Return	Max Drawdown	Sharpe Ratio	Sortino Ratio	Standard Deviation	Correlation with Benchmark
Screen	758.79%	15.42%	-67.28%	0.43	0.59	26.78%	0.65
SPDR S&P 500 ETF Trust	95.44%	4.57%	-55.42%	0.03	0.04	20.42%	-

©Portfolio123.com

HEDGED SIMULATION

Fig 11.2: Simulation data and equity curve: S&P 500 Materials, Hedged

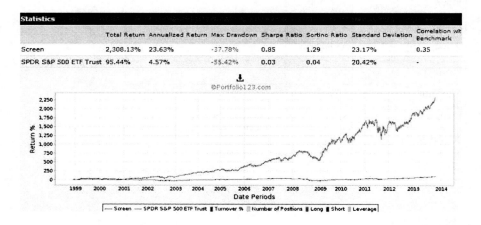

Statistics							
	Total Return	Annualized Return	Max Drawdown	Sharpe Ratio	Sortino Ratio	Standard Deviation	Correlation wit Benchmark
Screen	2,308.13%	23.63%	-37.78%	0.85	1.29	23.17%	0.35
SPDR S&P 500 ETF Trust	95.44%	4.57%	-55.42%	0.03	0.04	20.42%	-

CONSISTENCY

Annualised returns with hedging by five-year periods:

Table 11.4: Consistency over five-year periods

Period	1/2/1999–1/1/2004	1/1/2004–1/1/2009	1/1/2009–1/1/2014
Annualised return	24%	20%	26%

COMMENT

In this cyclical sector, a protection tactic is necessary in market downturns to avoid excessive losses. Like in some other cyclical sectors, in the hedged version the five-year annualised returns are very stable.

RUSSELL 2000 STRATEGY

INDIVIDUALLY RELEVANT FACTORS

Here are the factors from my working list that are individually relevant for the Russell 2000 Materials reference set:

Table 11.5: Individually relevant factors: Russell 2000 Materials

PS	Price to Sales Ratio, TTM
PB	Price to Book Ratio, Last Quarter
PFCF	Price To Free Cash Flow Per Share Ratio, TTM
S5YG	Sales Growth Rate, 5 Year (%)

STRATEGY DESCRIPTION

This time, the strategy is similar to the large cap one.

Table 11.6: Strategy description: Russell 2000 Materials

Name	Materials-R2000
Index	Russell 2000
Sector	Materials
Rebalanced	4 weeks
Positions	20
Maximum size	5%
Rules	Select the 20 stocks with the lowest PFCF
Transaction costs	0.5%

As in the S&P 500 version, the rationalised interpretation is to select cheap stocks regarding the price to free cash flow ratio.

Fig 11.3: Simulation data and equity curve: Russell 2000 Materials

Statistics

	Total Return	Annualized Return	Max Drawdown	Sharpe Ratio	Sortino Ratio	Standard Deviation	Correlation Benchmark
Screen	1,216.30%	18.75%	-74.24%	0.50	0.69	29.72%	0.63
SPDR S&P 500 ETF Trust	95.44%	4.57%	-55.42%	0.03	0.04	20.42%	-

HEDGED SIMULATION

Fig 11.4: Simulation data and equity curve: Russell 2000 Materials, Hedged

Statistics

	Total Return	Annualized Return	Max Drawdown	Sharpe Ratio	Sortino Ratio	Standard Deviation	Correlation Benchmark
Screen	3,659.36%	27.36%	-35.23%	0.89	1.34	26.12%	0.36
SPDR S&P 500 ETF Trust	95.44%	4.57%	-55.42%	0.03	0.04	20.42%	-

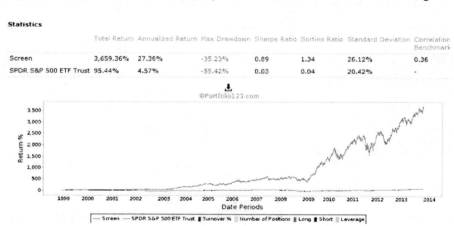

CONSISTENCY

Annualised returns with hedging by five-year periods:

Table 11.7: Consistency over five-year periods

Period	1/2/1999–1/1/2004	1/1/2004–1/1/2009	1/1/2009–1/1/2014
Annualised return	21%	19%	45%

COMMENT

In Materials, the small cap portfolio brings a better return than large caps for a similar risk, which makes the hedged version of Materials-R2000 attractive in spite of the additional liquidity risk. The five-year annualised returns of the first and second five-year periods are around 20% in the hedged version, and even above 40% for the last period.

CHAPTER 12

TELECOMMUNICATION SERVICES

SECTOR OVERVIEW

DEFINITION

Here is the GICS® definition by MSCI and Standard & Poor's:

> The Telecommunication Services Sector contains companies that provide communications services primarily through a fixed-line, cellular or wireless, high bandwidth and/or fiber optic cable network.

COMPANIES

This sector contains six companies in the S&P 500 and 25 in the Russell 2000. It is the smallest sector in company number. Here is the list of the S&P 500 companies:

Table 12.1: Stock examples: S&P 500 Telecommunication

Ticker	Name	Industry
CCI	Crown Castle International Corp	Wireless Telecommunication Services
CTL	CenturyLink Inc	Diversified Telecommunication Services
FTR	Frontier Communications Corp	Diversified Telecommunication Services
T	AT&T Inc	Diversified Telecommunication Services
VZ	Verizon Communications Inc	Diversified Telecommunication Services
WIN	Windstream Holdings Inc	Diversified Telecommunication Services

This set of stocks is too small for elaborate statistical strategies. For this sector, I therefore propose a unique strategy with 10 holdings in the Russell 3000 index. At the time I write this, there are 39 telecommunication services companies in the Russell 3000.

RUSSELL 3000 STRATEGY

INDIVIDUALLY RELEVANT FACTORS

Here are the factors from my working list that are individually relevant for the Russell 3000 Telecom reference set:

Table 12.2: Individually relevant factors: Russell 3000 Telecommunication

FPE	Next Year Projected PE Ratio
PFCF	Price To Free Cash Flow Per Share Ratio, TTM
ROA	Return on Assets, TTM (%)
GM	Gross Margin, TTM (%)

STRATEGY DESCRIPTION

This strategy uses a single valuation ratio.

Table 12.3: Strategy description: Russell 3000 Telecommunication

Name	Telecom-R3000
Index	Russell 3000 (= Russell 1000 + Russell 2000)
Sector	Telecommunication Services
Rebalanced	4 weeks
Positions	10
Maximum size	10%
Rules	Select the 10 companies with the lowest FPE
Transaction costs	0.5%

Rationalised interpretation: this strategy selects the cheapest companies relative to earnings estimate. The telecom sector was globally the hardest hit in the dot-com crash: taking all Russell 3000 Telecom stocks in equal weight, it is the only sector that is still in drawdown since the 2000 bubble.

BASIC SIMULATION

Fig 12.1: Simulation data and equity curve: Russell 3000 Telecommunication

Statistics

	Total Return	Annualized Return	Max Drawdown	Sharpe Ratio	Sortino Ratio	Standard Deviation	Correlation Benchmark
Screen	257.24%	8.86%	-61.54%	0.18	0.26	26.78%	0.59
SPDR S&P 500 ETF Trust	95.44%	4.57%	-55.42%	0.03	0.04	20.42%	-

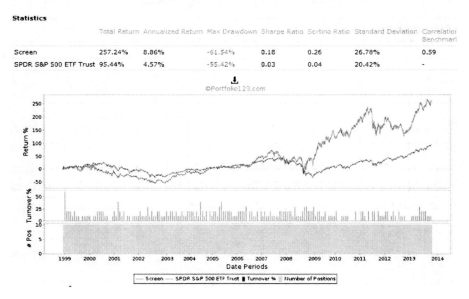

HEDGED SIMULATION

Fig 12.2: Simulation data and equity curve: Russell 3000 Telecommunication, Hedged

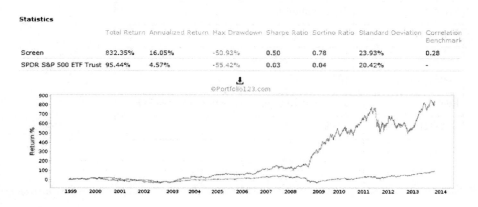

Statistics

	Total Return	Annualized Return	Max Drawdown	Sharpe Ratio	Sortino Ratio	Standard Deviation	Correlation Benchmark
Screen	832.35%	16.05%	-50.93%	0.50	0.78	23.93%	0.28
SPDR S&P 500 ETF Trust	95.44%	4.57%	-55.42%	0.03	0.04	20.42%	-

©Portfolio123.com

CONSISTENCY

Annualised returns with hedging by five-year periods:

Table 12.4: Consistency over five-year periods

Period	1/2/1999–1/1/2004	1/1/2004–1/1/2009	1/1/2009–1/1/2014
Annualised return	7%	27%	22%

COMMENT

Telecommunication Services are not only the smallest sector, but also the least profitable for at least 15 years. Compared with the whole Telecom sector, this strategy avoided the worst of the bursting of the dot-com bubble. That might also help in a possible bubble 2.0. In addition, the two last five-year periods have an annualised return above 20% (hedged), which is quite encouraging.

CHAPTER 13

UTILITIES

SECTOR OVERVIEW

DEFINITION

Here is the GICS® definition by MSCI and Standard & Poor's:

> The Utilities Sector comprises utility companies such as electric, gas and water utilities. It also includes independent power producers & energy traders and companies that engage in generation and distribution of electricity using renewable sources.

COMPANIES

This sector contains 30 companies in the S&P 500 and 35 in the Russell 2000. Here is the list of the 10 largest capitalisations at the time of writing, arranged in alphabetical order by ticker:

Table 13.1: Stock examples: S&P 500 Utilities

Ticker	Name	Industry
AEP	American Electric Power Co Inc	Electric Utilities
D	Dominion Resources Inc.	Multi-Utilities
DUK	Duke Energy Corp	Electric Utilities
EXC	Exelon Corp	Electric Utilities
NEE	NextEra Energy Inc	Electric Utilities
PCG	PG&E Corp	Multi-Utilities
PEG	Public Service Enterprise Group Inc	Multi-Utilities
PPL	PPL Corp	Electric Utilities
SO	Southern Co (The)	Electric Utilities
SRE	Sempra Energy	Multi-Utilities

S&P 500 STRATEGY

INDIVIDUALLY RELEVANT FACTORS

Here are the factors from my working list that are individually relevant for the S&P 500 Utilities reference set:

Table 13.2: Individually relevant factors: S&P 500 Utilities

S5YG	Sales Growth Rate, 5 Year (%)
CR	Current Ratio, Last Quarter
GM	Gross Margin, TTM (%)

STRATEGY DESCRIPTION

This time I will use two rules on the same growth ratio.

Table 13.3: Strategy description: S&P 500 Utilities

Name	Utilities-SP500
Index	S&P 500
Sector	Utilities
Rebalanced	4 weeks
Positions	10
Maximum size	10%
Rules	1- Exclude stocks with S5YG<-5% 2- Select the 10 stocks with the lowest S5YG
Transaction costs	0.2%

This is a contrarian strategy because the second rule selects the companies with the weakest growth rate. But the first rule excludes companies that are significantly losing their market. The thinking behind this strange strategy is that among large Utilities companies, stability pays for the shareholder. In this reference set, the more boring the business, the better for investors. An element of importance is that this sector has a higher concentration of companies paying a high dividend.

BASIC SIMULATION

Fig 13.1: Simulation data and equity curve: S&P 500 Utilities

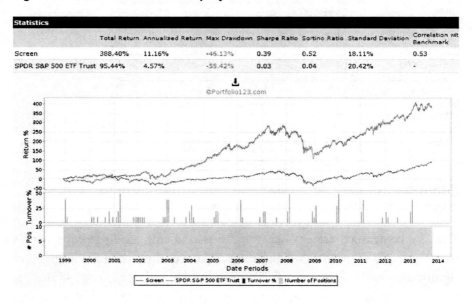

Statistics							
	Total Return	Annualized Return	Max Drawdown	Sharpe Ratio	Sortino Ratio	Standard Deviation	Correlation wit Benchmark
Screen	388.40%	11.16%	-46.13%	0.39	0.52	18.11%	0.53
SPDR S&P 500 ETF Trust	95.44%	4.57%	-55.42%	0.03	0.04	20.42%	-

HEDGED SIMULATION

Fig 13.2: Simulation data and equity curve: S&P 500 Utilities, Hedged

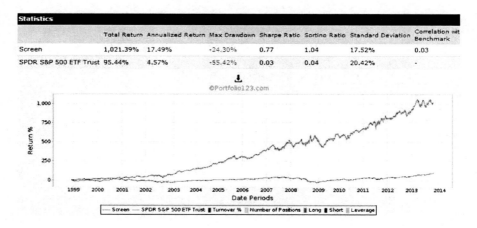

Statistics							
	Total Return	Annualized Return	Max Drawdown	Sharpe Ratio	Sortino Ratio	Standard Deviation	Correlation wit Benchmark
Screen	1,021.39%	17.49%	-24.30%	0.77	1.04	17.52%	0.03
SPDR S&P 500 ETF Trust	95.44%	4.57%	-55.42%	0.03	0.04	20.42%	-

CONSISTENCY

Annualised returns with hedging by five-year periods:

Table 13.4: Consistency over five-year periods

Period	1/2/1999–1/1/2004	1/1/2004–1/1/2009	1/1/2009–1/1/2014
Annualised return	19%	21%	13%

COMMENT

As a defensive sector, Utilities has a lower risk than cyclicals. The return is significantly lower than other defensive sectors: Consumer Staples and Health Care. All five-year annualised returns are above 10% (hedged), however a weaker return for the last period might be reason for caution.

RUSSELL 2000 STRATEGY

INDIVIDUALLY RELEVANT FACTORS

Here are the factors from my working list that are individually relevant for the Russell 2000 Utilities reference set:

Table 13.5: Individually relevant factors: Russell 2000 Utilities

PE	Price To Earnings Ratio Including Extraordinary Items, TTM
FPE	Next Year Projected PE Ratio
ROE	Return on Average Common Equity, TTM (%)
CR	Current Ratio, Last Quarter
NPM	Net Profit Margin, TTM (%)
INST	Institutional Percent Owned (%)

STRATEGY DESCRIPTION

I will use a single valuation ratio.

Table 13.6: Strategy description: Russell 2000 Utilities

Name	Utilities-R2000
Index	Russell 2000
Sector	Utilities
Rebalanced	4 weeks
Positions	20
Maximum size	5%
Rules	Select the 20 companies with the lowest FPE
Transaction costs	0.5%

The selection is focused on cheap companies regarding their projected earnings.

BASIC SIMULATION

Fig 13.3: Simulation data and equity curve: Russell 2000 Utilities

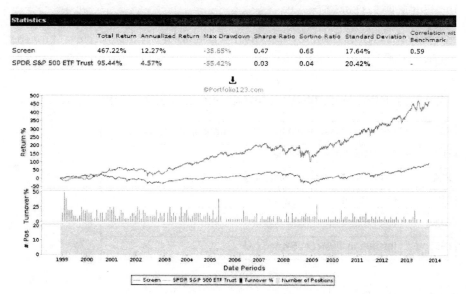

Statistics	Total Return	Annualized Return	Max Drawdown	Sharpe Ratio	Sortino Ratio	Standard Deviation	Correlation wit Benchmark
Screen	467.22%	12.27%	-35.65%	0.47	0.65	17.64%	0.59
SPDR S&P 500 ETF Trust	95.44%	4.57%	-55.42%	0.03	0.04	20.42%	-

HEDGED SIMULATION

Fig 13.4: Simulation data and equity curve: Russell 2000 Utilities, Hedged

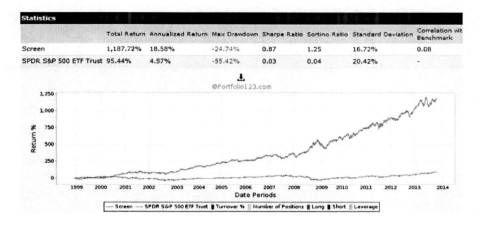

Statistics							
	Total Return	Annualized Return	Max Drawdown	Sharpe Ratio	Sortino Ratio	Standard Deviation	Correlation wit Benchmark
Screen	1,187.72%	18.58%	-24.74%	0.87	1.25	16.72%	0.08
SPDR S&P 500 ETF Trust	95.44%	4.57%	-55.42%	0.03	0.04	20.42%	-

CONSISTENCY

Annualised returns with hedging by five-year periods:

Table 13.7: Consistency over five-year periods

Period	1/2/1999–1/1/2004	1/1/2004–1/1/2009	1/1/2009–1/1/2014
Annualised return	22%	19%	16%

COMMENT

The small cap strategy has very similar characteristics to the S&P 500 portfolio. There is little incentive to take liquidity risk. All five-year annualised returns are above 15% (hedged), which is more encouraging.

CHAPTER 14

DOW JONES INDUSTRIAL AVERAGE

INDEX OVERVIEW

The DJIA contains 30 companies. Here is the list at the time of writing:

Table 14.1: Dow Jones Industrial Average Stocks

Ticker	Name	Sector
AXP	American Express Co	Financials
BA	Boeing Co (The)	Industrials
CAT	Caterpillar Inc	Industrials
CSCO	Cisco Systems Inc	Information Technology
CVX	Chevron Corp	Energy
DD	E. I. du Pont de Nemours and Co	Materials
DIS	Walt Disney Co (The)	Consumer Discretionary
GE	General Electric Co	Industrials
GS	Goldman Sachs Group Inc (The)	Financials
HD	Home Depot Inc. (The)	Consumer Discretionary
IBM	International Business Machines Corp	Information Technology
INTC	Intel Corp	Information Technology

Ticker	Name	Sector
JNJ	Johnson & Johnson	Health Care
JPM	JPMorgan Chase & Co	Financials
KO	Coca-Cola Co (The)	Consumer Staples
MCD	McDonald's Corp	Consumer Discretionary
MMM	3M Co	Industrials
MRK	Merck & Co Inc.	Health Care
MSFT	Microsoft Corp	Information Technology
NKE	Nike Inc	Consumer Discretionary
PFE	Pfizer Inc	Health Care
PG	Procter & Gamble Co (The)	Consumer Staples
T	AT&T Inc	Telecommunication Services
TRV	Travelers Companies Inc (The)	Financials
UNH	Unitedhealth Group Inc	Health Care
UTX	United Technologies Corp	Industrials
V	Visa Inc	Information Technology
VZ	Verizon Communications Inc	Telecommunication Services
WMT	Wal-Mart Stores Inc	Consumer Staples
XOM	Exxon Mobil Corp	Energy

DJ 30 STRATEGY

INDIVIDUALLY RELEVANT FACTORS

Here are the factors from my working list that are individually relevant for the DJ 30 reference set:

Table 14.2: Individually relevant factors: DJ 30

PE	Price To Earnings Ratio, Including Extraordinary Items, TTM
PEG	Price/Earnings to Next Year Growth Rate
PFCF	Price To Free Cash Flow Per Share Ratio, TTM
ROA	Return on Assets, TTM (%)
CR	Current Ratio, Quarterly
INST	Institutional Percent Owned, (%)

STRATEGY DESCRIPTION

For these very large companies, I will combine a valuation ratio and a profitability ratio.

Table 14.3: Strategy description: DJ 30

Name	DJ 30
Index	DJIA
Sector	All
Rebalanced	4 weeks
Positions	10
Maximum size	10%
Rules	1- Select the 20 companies with the lowest PE 2- Select the 10 companies with the highest ROA
Transaction costs	0.2%

In other words, this means excluding the 10 most expensive companies regarding the PE ratio, then keeping the 10 most profitable regarding the return on assets.

BASIC SIMULATION

Fig 14.1: Simulation data and equity curve: DJ 30

Statistics							
	Total Return	Annualized Return	Max Drawdown	Sharpe Ratio	Sortino Ratio	Standard Deviation	Correlation wit Benchmark
Screen	284.36%	9.39%	-41.61%	0.31	0.42	17.31%	0.71
SPDR S&P 500 ETF Trust	95.44%	4.57%	-55.42%	0.03	0.04	20.42%	-

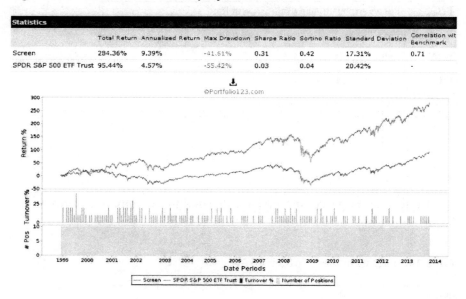

HEDGED SIMULATION

Fig 14.2: Simulation data and equity curve: DJ 30, Hedged

Statistics							
	Total Return	Annualized Return	Max Drawdown	Sharpe Ratio	Sortino Ratio	Standard Deviation	Correlation wit Benchmark
Screen	819.30%	15.94%	-23.18%	0.81	1.22	14.68%	0.22
SPDR S&P 500 ETF Trust	95.44%	4.57%	-55.42%	0.03	0.04	20.42%	-

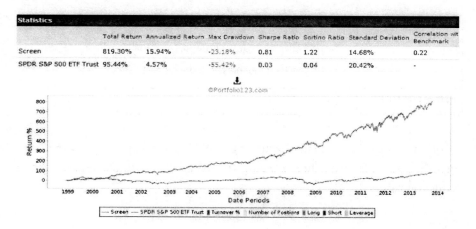

CONSISTENCY

Annualised returns with hedging by five-year periods:

Table 14.4: Consistency over five-year periods

Period	1/2/1999–1/1/2004	1/1/2004–1/1/2009	1/1/2009–1/1/2014
Annualised return	19%	15%	14%

COMMENT

This strategy is not the best, but it is impressive if we consider that it permanently holds one-third of the major and oldest US index. Five-year annualised returns are steady, from 13% to 20% (hedged). This is the most liquid strategy in the book – the average daily trading turnover of any DJ 30 stock is above $200 million.

To give a comparison, I have simulated a monthly version of the famous "Dogs of the Dow" strategy. It consists in selecting every four weeks the 10 stocks with the highest dividend yield (the original strategy is based on an annual rotation). The monthly Dogs of the Dow with my hedging tactics gives on the same period an average annual return of 15% (vs. 16% for our "lazy" DJ 30), a max drawdown of -34% (-23% for us) and a standard deviation of 17% (15% for us).

Our DJ 30 portfolio has a slightly higher return, and is significantly safer regarding drawdown and volatility. This conclusion is limited to the last 15 years, no claim is made for a longer period or for the future. Both strategies are comparable: they can be executed in a few minutes without the help of software, and have the same number of holdings in the same reference set.

CHAPTER 15

BENCHMARKING BY SECTORS

In the previous chapters the strategies were compared to a single benchmark: the S&P 500 Index. In this chapter they will be compared to sector indices.

Two series of indices will be used: the first one is static and capital-weighted, the second one is dynamic and based on a quantitative model. Comparing strategies with sector-based benchmarks is a more accurate way to judge them individually. Data are taken not directly from the indexes, but from ETFs based on them. Transaction and management costs are included on both sides, giving a realistic comparison from an investor's point of view.

S&P SELECT SECTOR INDEXES

DEFINITION

The following definition is an interpretation of information publicly available on the website **spindices.com**. A complete methodology document can be downloaded from this website.

All components of the S&P 500 are classified in their respective GICS sector, except for the Telecommunication Services sector which is grouped with Information Technology.

As a consequence:

- These indexes are based on the same classification as the S&P 500 lazy strategies, with the exception that IT also contains telecommunication stocks.

- They are more diversified as they hold all stocks in each sector.

- They are static: the membership is linked to the S&P 500 membership. A company enters or exits a sector index when it enters or exits the global index.

ETFS

The Select Sector SPDR Fund series aims at replicating, before expenses, the price and yield performance of these indexes. Here are the tickers by GICS sectors:

Table 15.1: Tickers of the Select Sector SPDR Fund series for GICS sectors

GICS sector	Ticker
Consumer Discretionary	XLY
Consumer Staples	XLP
Energy	XLE
Financials	XLF
Health Care	XLV
Industrials	XLI
Information Technology	XLK
Materials	XLB
Utilities	XLU

The annual net expense ratio is 0.17%. The nine ETFs have traded since 16 December 1998, which allows for a comparison on the whole backtest period.

PERFORMANCES

The following bar charts compare the non-hedged S&P 500 lazy strategies with the corresponding sector ETFs for the period 1/1/1999 to 1/1/2014. (A table in Appendix 3 gives the underlying numbers.)

Fig 15.1: Comparison of returns for lazy strategies v S&P Select Sector ETFs

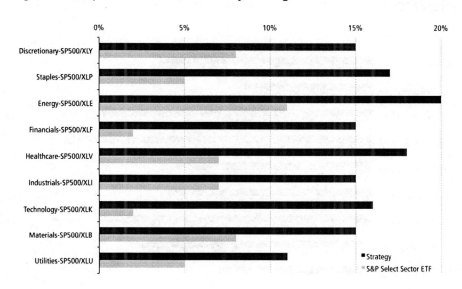

It can be seen in Fig 15.1 that all the S&P 500 lazy strategies have superior annualised returns than their benchmarks. The minimum additional annualised return is 6%. The Financials and Information Technology sectors have the best results: more than 14% of additional annualised return.

Looking at Fig 15.2, lazy strategies have a lower or equal risk (standard deviation) in five sectors: Consumer Discretionary, Consumer Staples, Materials and Utilities. When the risk is higher, the maximum difference in standard deviation is 4%.

Fig 15.2: Comparison of standard deviation for lazy strategies v S&P Select Sector ETFs

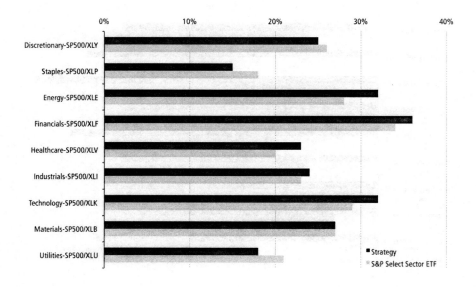

Fig 15.3: Comparison of max drawdown for lazy strategies v S&P Select Sector ETFs

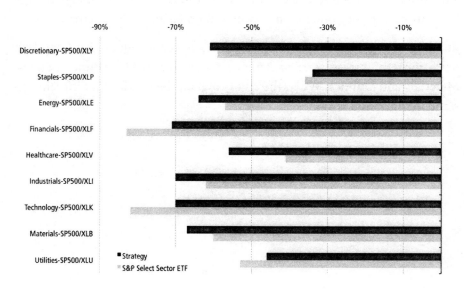

In five cases out of nine, lazy strategies have a deeper drawdown. The maximum difference in drawdown is 15% in Health Care.

The following bar chart compares the risk-adjusted returns measured by the Sortino ratio.

Fig 15.4: Comparison of Sortino ratios with static sector benchmarks

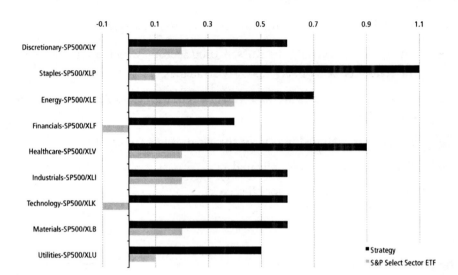

All the S&P 500 lazy strategies have a better risk-adjusted performance than their benchmarks. The minimum difference in Sortino ratio is 0.3.

AMEX STRATAQUANT INDEXES

DEFINITION

The following index methodology description is an interpretation of information publicly available on the website **nyse.com**. More details can be found on the websites of NYSE EURONEXT (**www.euronext.com**) and AMEX (**www.amex.com**).

Every quarter, all stocks in the Russell 1000 universe are given a growth score and a value score based on three price momentums and four quantitative fundamental factors. For a stock classified by Russell only as growth or only as value, the selection score is the score of its style. Otherwise, it is the best of both scores. In each sector, the bottom 25% is eliminated and the rest is ranked regarding the selection score and split into five subsets. The top subset has a capital allocation of 33.3%, the second has an allocation of 26.7%, the third has 20%, the fourth has 13.3%, the last has 6.7%. Within a subset, stocks have an equal weight.

There are notable differences with our lazy S&P 500 strategies:

- The reference sets are the Russell 1000 sectors, which are larger than the reference sets of S&P 500 lazy strategies.

- StrataQuant indexes are more diversified: they hold 75% of stocks in each sector.

- They are rebalanced quarterly, three times less frequently.

- The rules are more complicated.

- The rules are the same for all sectors.

ETFS

The First Trust AlphaDEX fund series aims at replicating, before expenses, the price and yield performance of the StrataQuant Indexes. Here is the list of tickers for the AlphaDEX funds by GICS sectors.

Table 15.2: Tickers of the AlphaDEX fund series for GICS sectors

AlphaDEX Fund	Ticker
Consumer Discretionary	FXD
Consumer Staples	FXG
Energy	FXN
Financials	FXO
Health Care	FXH
Industrials	FXR
Information Technology	FXL
Materials	FXZ
Utilities	FXU

The annual net expense ratio for the funds is 0.7%. The nine AlphaDEX ETFs have traded since 8 May 2007. This is a shorter period, however it does include a bear market (2008–2009) and a bull market (2009–2013).

PERFORMANCE

The following bar charts compare the non-hedged S&P 500 lazy strategies with the corresponding AlphaDEX sector ETFs for the period 5/8/2007 to 1/1/2014. A table in Appendix 3 gives the precise figures.

The logic of the bar charts is the same as in the previous section.

Fig 15.5: Comparison of returns for lazy strategies v AlphaDEX sector ETFs

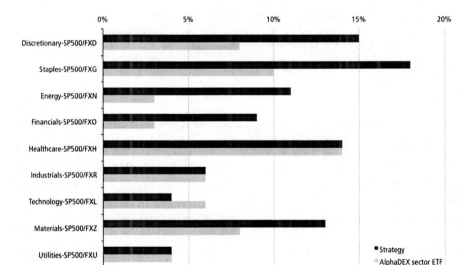

In spite of using simpler rules and a smaller set of stocks, almost all the S&P 500 lazy strategies have a better or equal annualised return than the respective AlphaDEX sector ETFs. The only exception is the Information Technology sector, with a relative loss of -1.3%. The best relative gain is in Consumer Staples and Energy with a 7.5% difference in annualised returns.

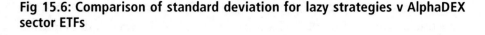

Fig 15.6: Comparison of standard deviation for lazy strategies v AlphaDEX sector ETFs

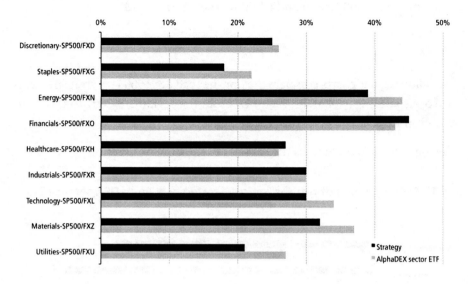

Even more interesting, the volatility (standard deviation) of lazy strategies is mostly below the volatility of corresponding AlphaDEX funds, despite having fewer holdings. When lazy strategies have a higher volatility (Financials, Health Care and Industrials), the maximum difference is 1.3%. When lazy strategies are less volatile, the maximum difference in volatility is 6.5%. It represents a significantly lower risk.

Looking at Fig 15.7, in four cases out of nine, lazy strategies have a deeper drawdown. The maximum difference in drawdown is 19% in Health Care.

Fig 15.7: Comparison of max drawdown for lazy strategies v AlphaDEX sector ETFs

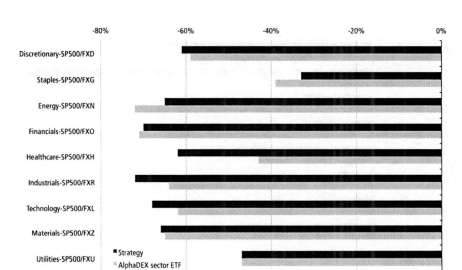

The following chart reports the Sortino ratios (no visible bar means ratio=0).

The S&P 500 lazy strategies have a better Sortino ratio than the AlphaDEX ETFs for five sectors. In the four other sectors they are equal. The largest advantage is in Consumer Staples.

Fig 15.8: Comparison of Sortino ratio for lazy strategies v AlphaDEX sector ETFs

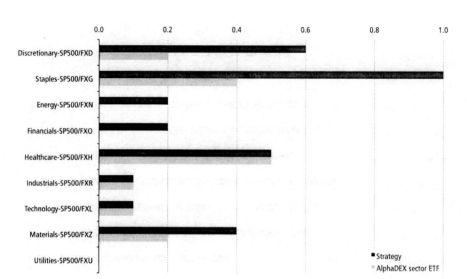

PART II SUMMARY

- Part II presented 20 stock strategies whose 15-year annualised returns are between 9% and 26%, whereas the return of the S&P 500 Index on the same period was 4.6%. All returns are calculated with dividends reinvested and including trading costs.

- Adding the hedging tactics defined in Part I, the annualised returns increase between 16% and 35%.

- The best returns are in Energy for large caps and in Health Care for small caps.

- The best risk-adjusted performances are in Consumer Staples for large caps and in Health Care for small caps.

- The most consistent returns in the hedged version (lowest difference between the best and worst five-year periods) is in Industrials for large caps and in Consumer Staples for small caps.

- All large cap strategies in their non-hedged versions are superior in return and risk adjusted performance to the Select Sector SPDR Fund series.

- Except in IT, all large cap strategies in their non-hedged versions are better or equivalent in return and risk adjusted performance to the First Trust AlphaDEX Fund series.

Part III proposes some applications for how to use these models to build a real portfolio.

PART III

APPLICATIONS

CHAPTER 16

COMBINED PORTFOLIOS

DEFINING GOALS AND CONSTRAINTS

There are many ways to use the previous strategies in real portfolios. A simple one is to combine two or more strategies. The best solution depends on each investor's goals and constraints, expressed in terms of:

- frequency and time available for portfolio management,
- capital invested,
- appetite for risk,
- aversion to market-timing or hedging,
- aversion or attraction to specific sectors,
- potential to trade in a margin account,
- economic data and personal opinions on sectors,
- other assets and incomes correlated with specific sectors.

This chapter shows two examples adapted to different situations.

1. 10 STOCK DEFENSIVE PORTFOLIO

This is a portfolio adapted to manage capital under $100K.

Table 16.1: Strategy description: Defensive-SP500

Name	Defensive-SP500
Index	S&P 500
Sector	Consumer Staples, Health Care
Rebalanced	4 weeks
Positions	10
Maximum size	10%
Rules	1- List the 20 stocks of Staples-SP500 and Healthcare-SP500
	2- Select the 10 stocks with the lowest market capitalisation
Transaction costs	0.2%

Fig 16.1: Simulation data and equity curve: Defensive-SP500

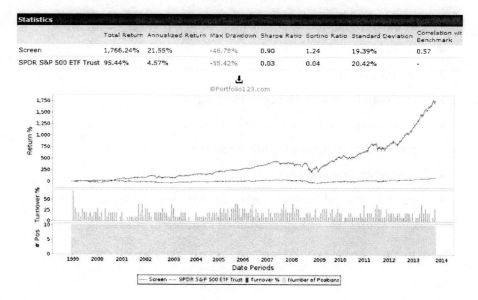

	Total Return	Annualized Return	Max Drawdown	Sharpe Ratio	Sortino Ratio	Standard Deviation	Correlation with Benchmark
Screen	1,766.24%	21.55%	-46.78%	0.90	1.24	19.39%	0.57
SPDR S&P 500 ETF Trust	95.44%	4.57%	-55.42%	0.03	0.04	20.42%	-

COMMENT

This looks a good solution for investors who want to invest only in very liquid stocks and are not attracted to market-timing and/or hedging. As it uses two defensive sectors, the drawdown is smoother than for the benchmark, but it is still deep. Of course, it is also possible to hedge this portfolio.

2. DIVERSIFIED PORTFOLIO QUARTERLY REBALANCED

This solution is adapted for an investor wanting to manage his/her portfolio only once per quarter, with capital above $100K.

Table 16.2: Strategy description: Diversified-Quarterly

Name	Diversified-Quarterly
Index	S&P 500, Russell 2000
Sector	Consumer Staples, Energy, Health Care, Industrials
Rebalanced	3 months
Positions	40
Maximum size	2.5%
Rules	Select the stocks of Staples-SP500, the stocks of Energy-SP500, the 10 best ranked stocks of Healthcare-R2000, the 10 best ranked stocks of Industrials-R2000.
Transaction costs	0.3%

Fig 16.2: Simulation data and equity curve: Diversified-Quarterly

Statistics								
	Total Return	Annualized Return	Max Drawdown	Sharpe Ratio	Sortino Ratio	Standard Deviation	Correlation wit Benchmark
Screen	3,431.19%	26.83%	-48.82%	1.00	1.30	22.81%	0.67
SPDR S&P 500 ETF Trust	95.44%	4.57%	-55.42%	0.03	0.04	20.42%	-

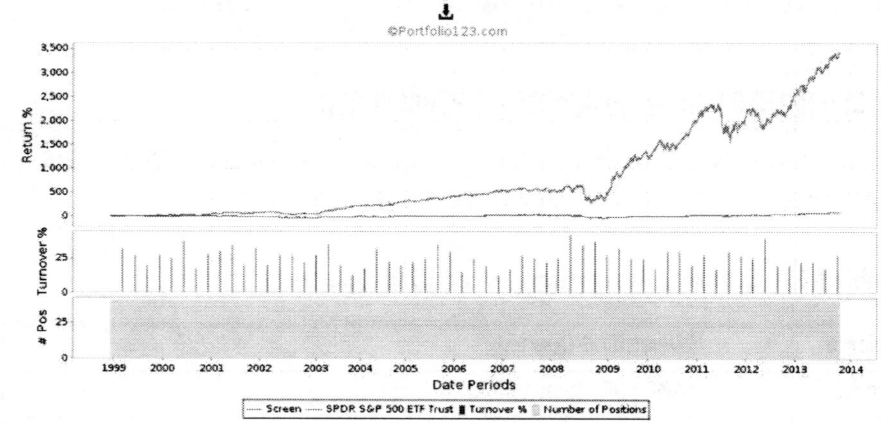

COMMENT

This portfolio is diversified by market capitalisation (half large caps, half small caps) and by sector (half defensive, half cyclical). Each position represents only 2.5% of the capital, which limits the idiosyncratic risk. No more than 25% of the capital is invested in a single sector.

It is interesting to note that thanks to a wider diversification a quarterly rebalancing gives a better performance than a four-week rebalancing when trading costs are taken into account. It is possible to hedge, but in this case the hedging position must be managed monthly or weekly to offer real protection. Even without that, this combined portfolio offers good Sharpe and Sortino ratios, especially for a quarterly strategy.

CHAPTER 17

OTHER APPLICATIONS

The lazy strategies can also be an entry point for investors who are not so lazy and have the time and skills to do additional work. If followed with discipline, using a set of quantitative models over the long term is probably the best way to get a steady and profitable performance, which can be improved by adding some discretionary analysis.

QUICK CHECK-UP

An investor faithfully following four or five strategies like those presented in my two books has a serious edge to beat the market in the long term. But for those who have a couple of extra hours every month I recommend doing a quick check-up of the selected stocks.

The quick check-up is a permissive elimination process. When one of the selected stocks has an ugly chart or very bad news, it may be profitable to eliminate it. I recommend eliminating a stock if it has a very bad period, but if there is some doubt then keep it in the selection. That is usually what I do for more sophisticated strategies in my portfolio and newsletter: when a stock looks really bad at first glance, I exclude it from my selection for the current week, and I take the next one in my ranking.

For example, I ran the Staples-R2000 model on 3/31/2014. Here is the list of tickers I obtained:

BGS, BREW, CALM, COKE, FARM, IMKTA, LFVN, LNCE, NATR, OME, REV, RNDY, SAM, SNAK, SPTN, SYUT, TIS, USNA, VGR, VLGEA.

I took a few minutes to look at the charts of the 20 stocks. I noted that two of them were in a downtrend on their daily charts and had broken supports on their weekly closing price: SYUT (Synutra International) and VLGEA (Village Super Market).

Some of the 18 other charts were not very nice, but these two really stood out as bad. For the four weeks starting 3/31/2014, the whole portfolio with 20 stocks returned -1.4%, with SYUT down -13.9% and VLGEA down -4.9%. Eliminating these two stocks and keeping the 18 others, the return was -0.5%, almost 1% better in four weeks. Of course, eliminating one or two stocks on discretionary criteria may not bring an advantage every time, but it may make a difference in the long term.

In a quick check-up I look at the following:

1. the daily candlestick chart,
2. the weekly candlestick chart, and
3. headings of the latest articles published on financial websites. If one looks especially negative, I read it quickly to figure out if it is fact or opinion.

Nothing more. Various financial websites give all the information publicly available about a stock. My preference is for **finviz.com**, which aggregates everything on a single page.

If you don't know anything about chart patterns and candlesticks, it may be better to just follow the chosen models. This is just a potential enhancement for some investors.

DEEPER ANALYSIS

More and more professional analysts use screeners to select candidates for a full analysis. In this case the lazy analysis may be a prelude to the real work, including due diligence research. Pre-selection models may simplify and accelerate the investment decision process.

All strategies listed here can serve this purpose. They specialise the pre-selection by sector. This may be an advantage for fund managers and professional investors who have sector-based diversification rules for their portfolios.

TOP-DOWN STRATEGIES

Tactical allocation is a concept aimed at performance optimisation by selecting or overweighting asset types (e.g. sectors) that are expected to outperform in the near future.

It may be profitable to mix tactical allocation and sector-based models in a top-down approach. The "top" part is the choice of one or several sectors; the "down" part is the selection of individual stocks inside these sectors.

Each sector is influenced by economic cycles of different and variable lengths. Theories of economic cycles are numerous and complicated. Their superposition sometimes shows a clear trend, sometimes it is chaotic. Selecting the right sectors is not an easy task. The choice may be discretionary, based on an evaluation of the current market cycles and qualitative analysis. It may also be based on quantitative elements like valuation ratios, price momentum, or other relative strength measures.

Once a set of sectors is selected in the higher part of the decision process, an investing choice can be made in the lower part: for example sector ETFs, or lazy strategies (see following illustration).

My previous book *Quantitative Investing* details an example of a tactical allocation strategy for sectors using simple technical analysis. Most tactical allocation strategies use ETFs or Futures contracts on specialised indexes.

We saw in Chapter 15 that the lazy strategies outperformed the corresponding ETFs. The idea of this top-down approach is to replace ETFs with our lazy portfolios in a tactical allocation framework. It should be able to produce a better performance. I write "should" because finance is in the realm of complexity. A property of, and indeed the very definition of a complex system, is that you may not be able to predict its behaviour from the behaviours of its parts.

Fig 17.1: Top-Down Approach

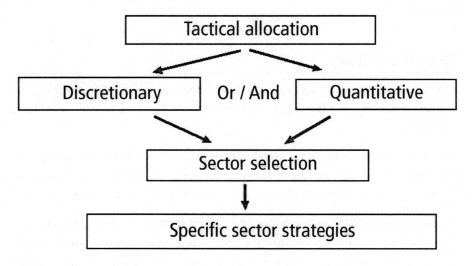

PART III SUMMARY

A defensive portfolio on 10 positions mixing two strategies is proposed. It is suitable for a capital under $100K.

A more diversified portfolio on 40 positions mixing four strategies and rebalanced only once every three months is proposed to manage a capital over $100K.

The last sections discuss mixing the sector-based strategies presented here with discretionary analysis or tactical allocation.

CONCLUSION

We are at the end of the book. All data presented here are historical, and the classic disclaimer says that past performance is not a guarantee for the future. However, with a correct methodology studying past performance is probably the best way we have to plan for the future. I have explained the methodology; I let you judge if it is correct or not.

There is no need to buy specific software to implement and execute the strategies described in this book. Various screeners can do the job. I can offer readers an extended free trial of Portfolio123 including access to the code of strategies in this book. For more information go to **stratecode.com**.

APPENDIX 1: LEVERAGED ETFS

Leveraged ETFs may help reduce the margin need and the cost of hedging. They are primarily instruments for short-term traders and have a bad reputation among investors because of their decay: leveraged ETFs often fall in price even when the underlying asset comes back to the same price. But this decay is not systematic.

UNDERSTANDING BETA-SLIPPAGE

The reason for the price decay is beta-slippage.

To understand this, imagine a very volatile asset that goes up 25% one day and down 20% the day after. A perfect double leveraged ETF goes up 50% the first day and down 40% the second day. On the second day, the underlying asset is back to its initial price:

$$(1 + 0.25) \times (1 - 0.2) = 1$$

Here is what happens to the 2x leveraged ETF:

$$(1 + 0.5) \times (1 - 0.4) = 0.9$$

Whereas the underlying asset is back to the same price, the 2x leveraged ETF is down 10%. Beta-slippage is not a scam. It is the normal mathematical behaviour of a leveraged and rebalanced portfolio. It depends on a specific sequence of gains and losses.

Beta-slippage is not always a decay: in a trending market, it can be positive. Imagine an asset going up 10% two days in a row. On the second day, the asset has gone up 21%:

$$(1 + 0.1) * (1 + 0.1) = 1.21$$

What happens to the 2x leveraged ETF:

$$(1 + 0.2) * (1 + 0.2) = 1.44$$

It is up 44%, more than twice 21%.

A real example: from 11/25/2012 to 11/25/2013 the S&P 500 Index returned 28% and UPRO (3x S&P 500 ETF) returned 114%. Intuitively, the return of UPRO should have been 28% x 3 = 84%. This is an additional 30% gain in 12 months.

Another example: from 11/1/2010 to 4/30/2011, SLV (silver ETF) returned 81% and AGQ (leveraged silver 2x ETF) returned 195%. Intuitively, AGQ should have returned 81% x 2 = 162%. This is an additional 33% gain in six months.

COMPARING S&P 500 ETFS FOR HEDGING

The following table lists ETFs that can be used to short the S&P 500. It gives the position to take in direction and size to hedge 100% of a portfolio.

Table A1.1: Possible ETFs for hedging

ETF	Type	Trade	Position size/portfolio value
SPY	Long 1x	Sell Short	100%
SH	Short 1x	Buy	100%
SSO	Long 2x	Sell Short	50%
SDS	Short 2x	Buy	50%
UPRO	Long 3x	Sell Short	33.3%
SPXU	Short 3x	Buy	33.3%

Only SPY was available before 2006, so using synthetic data calculated back to 1999 I have simulated the return of the optimistic hedging previously defined, with a decision every four weeks.

The next table gives the total returns of the hedging position between 1/2/1999 and 1/1/2014, taking into account a 0.1% rate for transaction costs. This return must be combined with the return of the portfolio itself. For the same period, a permanent long position in SPY has returned 4.6%.

Table A1.2: Hedging performance of S&P 500 ETFs

ETF	Total return of the hedging position (optimistic timing)
SPY (short)	105%*
SH (long)	121%
SSO (short 50%)	111%*
SDS (long 50%)	106%
UPRO (short 33.3%)	136%*
SPXU (long 33.3%)	104%

* Taking into account borrowing rates for short selling.

Since 1999, the hedging position with an optimistic timing delivers a profit with all these ETFs. UPRO is the best, but the annualised difference is only 1.5% between the best and the worst. If borrowing rates go up, SH may become the best solution. If the reason for using them is to reduce the margin, SDS and SPXU may be preferred.

APPENDIX 2: STRATEGY RETURNS

Table A2.1 summarises the 15-year annualised returns of the 20 strategies, with and without hedging.

Table A2.1: Strategy summary

	Name	Annualised return %	Annualised return, hedged %
1	Discretionary-SP500	15	23
2	Discretionary-R2000	22	31
3	Staples-SP500	17	23
4	Staples-R2000	17	24
5	Energy-SP500	20	29
6	Energy-R2000	20	29
7	Financials-SP500	16	24
8	Financials-R2000	14	22
9	Healthcare-SP500	18	26
10	Healthcare-R2000	26	35
11	Industrials-SP500	15	24
12	Industrials-R2000	23	33
13	Tech-SP500	16	24
14	Tech-R2000	23	31

	Name	Annualised return %	Annualised return, hedged %
14	Tech-R2000	23	31
15	Materials-SP500	14	24
16	Materials-R2000	19	27
17	Telecom-R3000	9	16
18	Utilities-SP500	11	17
19	Utilities-R2000	12	19
20	DJ 30	9	16

APPENDIX 3: AGAINST BENCHMARK

Tables of compared performance with benchmarks, by sector. Table A3.1 uses the static ETFs (1/1/1999 to 1/1/2014), Table A3.2 compares with the strategy-based AlphaDEX ETFs (5/8/2007 to 1/1/2014).

Table A3.1: Comparison with static sector benchmarks (1999–2014)

	Ann.Return	Max.Drawdown	Stand.Deviation	Sortino Ratio
Discretionary-SP500	15%	-61%	25%	0.6
XLY	8%	-59%	26%	0.2
Staples-SP500	17%	-34%	15%	1.1
XLP	5%	-36%	18%	0.1
Energy-SP500	20%	-64%	32%	0.7
XLE	11%	-57%	28%	0.4
Financials-SP500	15%	-71%	36%	0.4
XLF	2%	-83%	34%	-0.1
Healthcare-SP500	18%	-56%	23%	0.9
XLV	7%	-41%	20%	0.2
Industrials-SP500	15%	-70%	24%	0.6
XLI	7%	-62%	23%	0.2
Tech-SP500	16%	-70%	32%	0.6
XLK	2%	-82%	29%	-0.1
Materials-SP500	15%	-67%	27%	0.6
XLB	8%	-60%	27%	0.2
Utilities-SP500	11%	-46%	18%	0.5
XLU	5%	-53%	21%	0.1

Table A3.2: Comparison with dynamic sector benchmarks (2007–2014)

	Ann.Return	Max.Drawdown	Stand.Deviation	Sortino Ratio
Discretionary-SP500	12%	-60%	29%	0.4
FXD	8%	-65%	32%	0.2
Staples-SP500	18%	-33%	18%	1
FXG	10%	-39%	22%	0.4
Energy-SP500	11%	-65%	39%	0.2
FXN	3%	-72%	44%	0
Financials-SP500	9%	-70%	45%	0.2
FXO	3%	-71%	43%	0
Healthcare-SP500	14%	-62%	27%	0.5
FXH	14%	-43%	26%	0.5
Industrials-SP500	6%	-72%	30%	0.1
FXR	6%	-64%	30%	0.1
Tech-SP500	4%	-68%	30%	0.1
FXL	6%	-62%	34%	0.1
Materials-SP500	13%	-66%	32%	0.4
FXZ	8%	-65%	37%	0.2
Utilities-SP500	4%	-47%	21%	0
FXU	4%	-47%	27%	0

QUANTITATIVE INVESTING

Strategies to exploit stock market anomalies for all investors

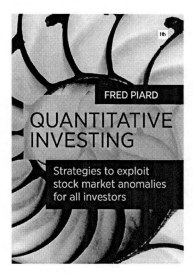

This book provides straightforward quantitative strategies that any investor can implement with little work using simple, free or low-cost tools and services.

But what exactly is quantitative investing?

There are various possible definitions of quantitative investing, but the author defines it as:

"Identifying reasonable and measurable hypotheses about behaviours of the financial market so as to make investment decisions with an acceptable confidence in expected returns and risks."

The main advantages in using quantitative models are that they:

- make the investment process independent of opinions and emotions (the most important factor for an individual investor), and

- make it reproducible by anyone at any time (the most important factor for a fund)

With a set of good strategies, quantitative investing allows one to act in the market at specific pre-planned times. It is possible to work on this just once a week or month, and ignore charts and the news. It removes most of the doubts and emotions with the discipline of keeping a long-term vision and sensible money management. This book will show you how.

Lightning Source UK Ltd.
Milton Keynes UK
UKOW05f0239120315

247679UK00003B/58/P